D1639341

Biblical, comprehensive and practical, this is a very welcome addition to the small number of books available for those who have recently become Christians. It is ideal to give to a new Christian, but also to be read by any believer who wants to be reminded of the great blessings and ongoing duties of the Christian life.

Rev. Jeremy Bailey,
Pastor of Bethlehem Evangelical Church, Port Talbot

❧

Clear. Concise. Comprehensive. Unwrapped is a great starting point for new Christians, but also a lovely refresher for long-standing believers. It's packed full of foundational information and practical advice, but it will also warm your heart. A delight.

Tim Chester,
Pastor of Grace Church Boroughbridge in North Yorkshire, and the author of over 40 books including *Enjoying God: Experience the Power of God in Everyday Life*.

❧

I highly commend Dr. John Blanchard's newest book, *Unwrapped!* as a worthy addition to his previous volumes which have benefited so many because of his faithfulness to the Word of God, his appealing style and compelling clarity. This particular volume will send you, like it did me, further down the road of obedience to our Savior as it equips us to be in the world but not "of the world." It also informs us how to tell the world of our Savior, the Lord Jesus Christ, who is no friend to sin but a glorious friend for sinners.

Dr. Harry L. Reeder, III
Pastor, Briarwood Presbyterian Church, Birmingham, AL, USA

UNWRAPPED!

Living the Christian life in today's world

JOHN BLANCHARD

EP BOOKS (Evangelical Press), Registered Office: 140 Coniscliffe Road, Darlington, Co Durham DL3 7RT

EP Books are distributed in the UK by 10ofthose.com.

admin@epbooks.org

www.epbooks.org

EP Books are distributed in the USA by:

JPL Books, 3883 Linden Ave. S.E., Wyoming, MI 49548

order@jplbooks.com

www.jplbooks.com

British Library Cataloguing in Publication Data available

Print ISBN 978-1-78397-253-1

eBook ISBN 978-1-78397-254-8

CONTENTS

INTRODUCTION

During a week of engagements on the Caribbean island of Grand Cayman I was invited to go snorkelling, something I had never done before. I jumped at the opportunity and one morning a small boat took me out into a lagoon. Putting on the diving mask, snorkel and flippers was no problem, though I did hesitate when told that I should then throw myself backwards over the side of the boat! Moments later, I could hardly believe my eyes. Everywhere I looked there were brilliantly-coloured anemones, sea stars, stingrays, tarpon, yellowtail and blue tangs, green turtles, sea urchins, coral morphs, and many other creatures I was seeing for the first time. I was in another world, and was reluctant to leave.

The Cayman experience came to mind as I began to write this book, because becoming a Christian means entering another world, not physically of course, but spiritually. The Bible even goes so far as to say that a person becoming a Christian is 'a new creation' because 'the old has passed away' and 'the new has come' (2 Corinthians 5:17). Because I have absolute confidence that the Bible is 'the living and abiding word of God' (1 Peter 1:23), I will be quoting it nearly 400 times and in Chapter 9 will explain why and how it is such an infallible guide to us as we go through life.

There are said to be over 4,000 different religions in today's world, and many people are confused, indifferent or unaware about what true Christianity is—and therefore about how to become a Christian and how to live as one. This is exactly why this book is being written, and why it has in mind not only those who have recently become Christians but also those who are further along in their spiritual journey.

The first six chapters of this book are largely doctrinal (explaining Christian beliefs), while those that follow are largely practical (showing how to live them out). There is an important reason for this. In his superb book *Know Your Christian Life,* the British Bible teacher Sinclair Ferguson writes, 'It is one of the facts of spiritual reality that practical Christian living is based on understanding and knowledge… how we think is one of the determining factors in how we live!'

My hope and prayer is that the following pages will give you a clear picture of some of Christianity's bedrock truths, then open a road map to guide you on your journey. It will be obvious from its size that the book does not deal in depth with any of the subjects it mentions. It is intended as a primer for those relatively new in the faith—and as a refresher course for those who have been Christians for some time—but it does pinpoint key subjects that stand out as Christianity is unwrapped.

Enjoy it!

John Blanchard, Banstead, Surrey
March 2019

❧ I ❧

THE DARK SKY

IT IS ESTIMATED that about 5,000 stars are visible to the unaided human eye from any one spot on earth, yet none can be seen in broad daylight. It is only when night falls that they can be seen in contrast to their jet-black background, and it is only when we understand people's spiritual condition before they become Christians that we get a clear picture of how brilliant Christianity really is.

SQUARE ONE

To get all of this in perspective we need to begin at the beginning. When God had completed creating the entire universe he pronounced it 'very good' (Genesis 1:31). When we realize that the One who said this is utterly perfect—'God is light, and in him is no darkness at all' (1 John 1:5)—it means that the whole universe, from the most gigantic galaxy to the tiniest organism or item, was absolutely flawless. This perfection included the first human beings; we are specifically told, 'So God created man in his own image, in the image of God he created him; male and female he created them'

(Genesis 1:27). This does not mean that they were the same size and shape, as God has neither—'God is spirit' (John 4:24)—but that they were created with the unique ability to have a living relationship with him. It is impossible to imagine the nature of life on our planet at that time. Our first parents lived in perfect relationships with their Creator, with each other, with every other created being, and with the entire cosmos. There was not the slightest blemish to be found anywhere.

It is not rocket science to see that things are very different now, and the Bible pinpoints the moment when everything went disastrously wrong. Our first parents' perfect relationships were dependent on their complete obedience to God, but at some point (we are not given any time line) they chose to rebel against him and to go their own way. When they did, 'sin came into the world' (Romans 5:12), with catastrophic, universal consequences. Their unique and perfect relationship with God was lost; their flawless love for each other was ruined; and for the first time they knew what it was to be guilty, alienated, ashamed and afraid. What is more, the whole of creation was thrown out of sync, with the result that it is now 'in bondage to decay' (Romans 8:21). Natural disasters such as hurricanes, tornados, tsunamis, floods and earthquakes give us dramatic evidence of this.

We have no space to develop this here, so we will concentrate on the effect our first parents' rebellious disobedience continues to have on the human race. Although he was created in God's perfect image, when the first man (Adam) began to produce children they were 'in his own likeness, *after his image*' (Genesis 5:3), inheriting both their father's physical nature and his sinful spiritual nature. Adam was not only the natural head of the human race, he was also its representative head, and when he sinned he did so as humanity's trustee. As the Bible puts it, 'By the one man's disobedience the many were made sinners' (Romans 5:19). Theologians call this 'original sin' and perhaps nothing in the Bible more clearly describes our spiritual condition by nature.

HELPLESS HUMANITY

The Bible underlines man's built-in crisis in a number of vivid ways. It says we were *lost:* 'All we like sheep have gone astray; we have turned every one to his own way' (Isaiah 53:6). It says we were *deaf*, so that we 'cannot listen' (Jeremiah 6:10) to God's voice; unless God intervenes, asking a person to understand spiritual truth is like asking someone who is stone deaf to interpret a piece of music. It says we were *blind*; that we were like those who 'grope at noonday, as the blind grope in darkness' (Deuteronomy 28:29) and that left to ourselves we 'cannot see the kingdom of God' (John 3:3). This explains why you may have heard the Christian gospel many times before you finally grasped its real meaning and responded to it. Even worse, it says that we were spiritually lifeless, 'dead in our trespasses [*one of the Bible's words for sinful actions*]' (Ephesians 2:5), so unable to do anything to contribute to our salvation (more of this in the next chapter). Countless people who have no interest in the Christian faith are capable of good social behavior, such as helping those in need, but this can never solve their basic spiritual problem, as their actions are not done out of love for God or a desire to please him.

Nor can taking part in religious activity solve the problem. Even Isaiah, one of the greatest prophets in the Bible, includes himself when he confesses, 'All our righteous deeds are like a polluted garment' (Isaiah 64:6). Looking back on his pre-Christian life, the apostle Paul says that he could easily have outdone anyone who boasted that they could get right with God by their own religious efforts, yet as a Christian he could now say, 'I count everything as loss because of the surpassing worth of knowing Christ Jesus my Lord' (Philippians 3:8).

Worst of all, we were 'by nature children of wrath' (Ephesians 2:3), rightly condemned by God's perfect holiness and justice. Having acknowledged that God's judgement was 'blameless', Israel's King David confesses, 'Behold, I was brought forth in iniquity, and in sin did my mother conceive me' (Psalm 51: 4-5). He was not accusing his mother (or his father for that matter) of being sinful in becoming his parents. Instead, he was acknowledging that like the rest of humanity he came from corrupted and polluted stock that stretched all the way back to Adam, which meant that he was not only a sinner by choice, but also by nature. He was saying that he inherited from all his predecessors a guilty, fallen nature and a fatal tendency to break God's law.

This cuts across most people's idea of what sin is. To some, it means gross wrongdoing such as murder, rape or child abuse. To others, it is just a religious idea or something invented by the church. But the Bible shows us the truth about sin. It describes it as a stain, a rebellion, a poison, crookedness, a burden, a storm, wandering, a sickness, a disease, a field of weeds, darkness, blindness, bondage, a debt, robbery and a curse. Sin is not trivial, but terrible, rebellion against our Maker. Sin is not superficial; it is something deep-rooted in the human heart, separating us from God and tainting everything we are and do. This means that left to ourselves we constantly and inevitably 'fall short of the glory of God' (Romans 3:23), and are unable to fulfil the purpose for which he created us, or to do anything to put things right. That is the dark sky Christians have left behind…

WHAT HAPPENED?

As we have now seen, everyone is guilty of breaking God's law, regardless of whether they know or admit it. God's perfect justice means we all deserve condemnation and punishment. The Bible gets straight to the point: 'For the wages of sin is death' (Romans 6:23), which is not only physical but spiritual death (eternal separation from the mercy and love of God). Only God could do something to remedy the situation—and he has!

The Bible's central message is that at the very point of man's utter helplessness, God intervened in the person of his eternal Son, the Lord Jesus Christ. One of his biblical titles is 'the last Adam' (1 Corinthians 15:45), because he came into the world to restore to man all that the first Adam lost when he fell into sin. Although Jesus was (and is) God, he became man, adding humanity to his deity. As the apostle John puts it, 'The Word [*another name for the second Person of the Trinity, see page 7 for more about this*] became flesh and dwelt among us' (John 1:14). As a man, he was subject to all the spiritual pressures we face today, yet he remained 'without sin' (Hebrews 4:15). Where Adam yielded, Jesus resisted;

where Adam fell, Jesus stood; where Adam failed, Jesus conquered.

But that was not all. Having resisted every attack of the devil, having never given way to temptation, having never once sinned, he then allowed himself to be put to death and take the place of guilty sinners by bearing in his own body and spirit God's righteous judgement against human sin. He did all of this so that people like you and me could be released from the condemnation and punishment our sin deserves and be brought into a right relationship with God. In Paul's amazing words, 'For our sake he [*God*] made him to be sin who knew no sin, so that in him we might become the righteousness of God' (2 Corinthians 5:21).

Yet even that is not the end of the story. On the third day Jesus rose from the dead, giving dynamic proof that his sacrificial death had paid in full the penalty for the sins of those in whose place he died. No wonder what God did in sending Jesus into the world is called 'the gospel,' or good news! This is the very heart of Christianity. Because of God's amazing love, guilty sinners can be declared righteous, set free from condemnation, enabled to live God-pleasing lives and be assured of spending eternity in God's glorious presence. If you are a Christian, these things are true of you —*but how did this happen?*

FROM DEATH TO LIFE

The opposite of death is life, and nothing else can take its place. Good works, religious activity, sincerity, and all the other things on which many people pin their hopes of getting right with God can no more overcome death than placing flowers on a coffin can bring a corpse back to life. Speaking to an influential religious leader, Jesus makes this crystal clear: 'Unless one is born again he cannot see the kingdom of God' (John 3:3). Needless to say, the religious leader was baffled by what Jesus told him, and asks, 'How can a man be born when he is old? Can he enter a second time into his mother's womb and be born?' (John 3:4). In response, Jesus explains that he was referring to a spiritual birth: 'That which is born of the flesh is flesh, and that which is born of the Spirit is spirit. Do not marvel that I said to you, "You must be born again"' (John 3:6-7). By 'the Spirit' Jesus meant the Holy Spirit, one of the three persons in the Godhead. While God is one in essence and nature, each of the three persons in the Godhead (God the Father, God the Son and God the Holy Spirit) is distinctly and equally divine. The Holy Spirit is not one of three gods, but one of three persons in the eternal Godhead. He is often referred to as the Third Person of the Holy Trinity, but this in no way means that he is inferior to the Father or the Son. The Holy Spirit is God—sovereign, eternal and divine—and is therefore to be worshipped, glorified, honoured and obeyed.

We will see more of what the Bible says about the Holy Spirit in Chapter 14, but the important thing to grasp here is that only *God* can bring about the life-giving transformation a spiritually dead person needs.

The new birth is a supernatural work of God, a miracle that can neither be explained nor controlled. If you are a Christian, it is not because God has rewarded you for your morality, sincerity, respectability or anything else. The Bible says that 'children of God' (one of the ways it describes Christians) are those whose new, spiritual birth was 'not of blood [*natural descent*], nor of the will of the flesh [*human desire*], nor of the will of man [*human determination*], but of God' (John 1:12-13). The new birth is not a matter of turning over a new leaf, but of taking in a new life. No Christian should ever tire of being grateful to God for this miracle, which has brought them into a living relationship with him that they could never otherwise have known. As Jesus puts it, a Christian is someone who 'has passed from death to life' (John 5:24).

REALITY CHECKS

We have already seen that the new birth is essential before anyone can enter the kingdom of God, but there is another qualification Jesus says is essential. When he hears people arguing over their relative importance, he tells them, 'Unless you turn and become like children, you will never enter the kingdom of heaven' (Matthew 18:3). This is usually called *conversion*, which can be recognized by two things, repentance and faith. As both words are often misunderstood, we need to look closely at them here.

Repentance is one of the most important subjects to which we could ever give attention. Jesus began his public ministry with the words, 'Repent, for the kingdom of heaven is at hand' (Matthew 4:17). When his disciples began preaching they 'went out and proclaimed that people should repent' (Mark 6:12), and in the course of his great sermon in Athens, the apostle Paul told his hearers that '[*God*] commands all people everywhere to repent' (Acts 17:30). This is enough to tell us that repentance is essential and vital.

Repentance is much more than regret or self-pity. Instead, it means a radical change of mind, heart and will. It is a change of *mind*, an acceptance that God is right in condemning human sin, and that there is no point in making excuses for our failures. As David told God, 'Against you, you only, have I sinned and done what is evil in your sight, so that you may be justified in your words and blameless in your judgement' (Psalm 51:4). Repentance is also a change of *heart*. It means being truly sorry for our sin, realizing its loathsomeness in God's sight. It is also a change of *will*, a serious determination to live in a way that is pleasing to God, instead of one governed by our own desires or preferences. A person repenting does not suddenly become perfect, yet the change is so radical that C. S. Lewis called it going 'full speed astern'.

Faith also involves a change of mind, heart and will. It is a change of *mind*. Not only does the Bible say that 'without faith it is impossible to please [*God*]' it adds, 'for whoever would draw near to God must believe that he exists and that he rewards those who seek him' (Hebrews 11:6). This is obvious and needs no explanation. But faith is also a change of *heart*, as the truth about God's love and Jesus' sacrificial death grips the Christian in a way that goes far beyond agreeing with historical facts: 'For with the heart one believes and is justified [*made right with God*]' (Romans 10:10). The apostle Paul testified to this when he wrote, 'The life I now live in the flesh I live by faith in the Son of God, who loved me and gave himself for me' (Galatians 2:20). Thirdly, faith involves the *will*. It is not merely a combination of facts and feelings, it is also personal commitment. We all exercise faith every day in many different ways, such as boarding an airplane, driving a car, putting money in a bank, or eating a meal in a restaurant. The faith that makes and marks a Christian is not consent to a proposition, but commitment to a person, the Lord Jesus Christ.

Repentance and faith can be seen as reality checks. They confirm for the Christian that the new birth has taken place —and the all-important thing for you to realize as you sense that they are your experience is that *they are God's gifts to you,* not things you have created for yourself. On what is often called the Christian church's birthday, the apostle Peter preached that after Jesus had died, God raised him from the dead and 'exalted him at his right hand as Leader and Saviour, to give repentance to Israel and forgiveness of sins'

(Acts 5:31). Later, after he had shared the gospel with those who were not Israelites, he reported to the church leaders in Jerusalem that 'God gave the same gift to them as he gave to us' (Acts 11:17). Faith in the Lord Jesus Christ is also a gift; Paul told the church at Ephesus, 'For by grace you have been saved through faith. And this is not your own doing; it is the gift of God, not a result of works, so that no one may boast' (Ephesians 2:8-9).

3

THE 'IMPOSSIBLE' FACT

THE DEATH and resurrection of Jesus bring tremendous blessings to those who become Christians by trusting him as their own personal Saviour. To see what these are means looking at some of the most important words in the New Testament. The first of these is so fundamental that it needs a chapter on its own.

When Jesus came to the earth, was born as a human being, lived a perfect life, died, and rose from the dead, he was doing so *on behalf of others.* As we saw in Chapter 2, the wages (that is, the penalty) for sin is death—and when Jesus died he was paying that penalty. Yet as Jesus was 'without sin' (Hebrews 4:15), why did he die? The Bible's amazing answer is that in his death he was paying the penalty *for other people's sins.* It tells us that he 'suffered once for sins, the righteous for the unrighteous, that he might bring us to God' (1 Peter 3:18). As the apostle John puts it, Jesus 'laid down his life for us' (1 John 3:16). In the most amazing act of love, he endured sin's ultimate penalty in the place of those who were exposed to God's righteous anger, and who would otherwise be exposed to that anger for ever.

RIGHT WITH GOD

This brings us to one of the longest words in the New Testament, and one of the most important in Christian doctrine. That being so, the time you spend reading (and if necessary, re-reading) this chapter will be well spent. The word is *'justification.'* It comes from the law courts, and is what takes place when a judge declares a person to be innocent in the eyes of the law. It would obviously be wrong for a judge to declare a person innocent if he knew them to be guilty, or guilty if he knew them to be innocent, and the Bible confirms this: 'He who justifies the wicked and he who condemns the righteous are both alike an abomination to the LORD' (Proverbs 17:15). Justification is the opposite of condemnation. It does not make the person concerned innocent or guilty, nor does it define or change their character in any way. Instead, a judge declares how the person before him stands *in relation to the law of the land.* Yet as we have already seen that in God's eyes we are all guilty law-breakers, condemned by nature and practice, our case would seem to be hopeless. How can we possibly be treated by him as if we had never broken his law?

It is exactly at this point that we come across one of the most amazing truths in the whole Bible: 'For God so loved the world, that he gave his only Son, that whoever believes in him should not perish but have eternal life' (John 3:16). Elsewhere, the same amazing truth is summarized like this: 'The Father has sent his Son to be the Saviour of the world' (1 John 4:14). The Son did not twist his Father's arm and persuade him to save sinners against his will. Instead, the plan of salvation is nothing less than the love of God in action.

In his perfect life, Jesus met all the demands of God's law —he 'committed no sin' (1 Peter 2:22)— yet in his death he paid in full the penalty it demands of those who break it. Jesus was punished as though he had never kept the law, so that those in whose place he died could be treated as though they had never broken it. Justified sinners are brought into God's favour and received as though they had met all the demands of God's holy law. As the apostle Paul confirms, 'Therefore, since we have been justified by faith, we have peace with God through our Lord Jesus Christ' (Romans 5:1). When we say that God justifies a person, we are not saying that he pronounces a guilty person to have been innocent all along (which would be untrue) but that he accepts what Jesus did on their behalf and in their place, and pardons the sinner on that basis.

The next amazing thing we discover about justification is that although it cost Jesus everything, it costs Christians nothing! The means of justification (the way in which a person receives it) is by faith alone, and that is a gift from God. As the apostle Paul puts it, Christians are 'justified by [*God's*] grace as a gift' (Romans 3:24). Yet millions of religious people have missed the whole wonderful truth of what the Bible is saying at this point. Often with great sincerity, they try to earn their justification. But there is no such thing as salvation by character; what people need is salvation *from* character. God promises salvation only to those who abandon trusting in their own efforts and cast themselves without reserve on Jesus and what he has done for them.

THE LAW AT WORK

This does not mean that God's law (the Ten Commandments, for instance) has no value. The Bible makes it clear that 'through the law comes knowledge of sin' (Romans 3:20). The law opens our eyes to the true nature of sin as rebellion against God, and to our own guilt in not keeping it. We could even say that it is because of God's grace that we have God's law! We should be grateful to God for this. But God's law has another purpose. The Bible says that although left to ourselves we are 'held captive under the law' (Galatians 3:23), it is intended 'to lead us to Christ' (Galatians 3:24, NIV). It shows us that only by trusting in someone who has kept it perfectly in every part can we escape the condemnation it brings—and Jesus came 'not to abolish the Law or the Prophets... but to fulfil them' (Matthew 5:17). This is something none of us has done. Even when we have tried our hardest, the smallest failure condemns us as lawbreakers. The Bible spells it out: 'For all who rely on works of the law are under a curse; for it is written, "Cursed be everyone who does not abide by *all things* written in the Book of the Law, and do them"' (Galatians 3:10). As another New Testament writer puts it, 'Whoever keeps the whole law but fails in one point has become accountable for all of it' (James 2:10). But the divine curse (condemnation and death) we deserve because of our disobedience was paid by Jesus, who 'redeemed us from the curse of the law by becoming a curse for us' (Galatians 3:13). God's law is still the perfect moral standard for the Christian life, but nobody becomes a Christian by his own efforts at keeping it.

One further, spine-tingling thing about justification needs to be added. So far, we have concentrated on the fact that in justification our sin is attributed to Jesus. Yet the equally amazing truth is that at the same time *Jesus' righteousness is credited to us,* so that in God's sight we are as perfectly righteous as Jesus himself! What is more, our justification is secure for ever. It can never be damaged, diminished or destroyed, which is why the apostle Paul can declare that he stands before God 'not having a righteousness of my own that comes from the law, but that which comes through faith in Christ' (Philippians 3:9).

Can guilty, rebellious sinners be accepted by a holy God as if they were as righteous as his son Jesus, who was 'holy, innocent, unstained, separated from sinners' (Hebrews 7:26)? The whole idea sounds impossible—but because of God's amazing love and grace it is true!

4

BIG WORDS—GREAT TRUTHS

WITH THE STUPENDOUS truth of justification in mind, we can now turn to some of the other great New Testament words that underpin what it means to be a Christian.

The first of these is *propitiation*. We may never use this word in everyday life, but it is hugely important. It means satisfying an offended person by paying the penalty they demand for an offence committed against them. The offended person can then receive back into favour the person who committed the offence. In many English versions of the Bible the original Greek word for 'propitiation' is translated 'atonement'. To 'atone' means to deal with an offence so that the offender and the person offended can be 'at one'. This is what Jesus did in dying on behalf of others: 'In this is love, not that we have loved God but that he loved us and sent his Son to be the propitiation for our sins' (1 John 4:10).

God has zero tolerance of sin, and his holiness demands that all sin be punished. When Jesus became accountable for the sins of others he was punished as though he had been responsible for them, and he bore that punishment in full.

When in his dying agony he cried out, 'My God, my God, why have you forsaken me?' (Matthew 27:46), it did not mean that God was not there (as God is always everywhere), but that in his righteous anger against the sin Jesus was bearing, God inflicted the ultimate penalty.

The next word is fairly familiar: *ransom*. We often hear of terrorists or other kidnappers taking prisoners and then demanding a ransom for their release. The Bible teaches that sinners are not merely captive to their own ungodly ideas, but that they are in 'the snare of the devil, after being captured by him to do his will' (2 Timothy 2:26). Jesus came to deal with this situation and to 'give his life as a ransom for many' (Mark 10:45). His death on the cross paid the ransom price rightly demanded by a holy God, so that God's justice could be satisfied and the sinners in whose place Jesus died could be set free.

Next comes *redemption*. When a ransom has been paid, the captives are set free, or redeemed, and this is what happens to those who trust in Jesus, who 'redeemed us from the curse of the law by becoming a curse for us' (Galatians 3:13). By nature we are under the 'curse' of God's holy law, which pronounces us guilty in his sight. Jesus was under no such curse, yet in order to satisfy the demands of God's justice he bore the curse of the law in full, setting us free to live in a way that is pleasing to God.

Forgiveness is a word we commonly use, and we are all familiar with the idea of forgiving (or being forgiven), even if an apology is sometimes asked for first, but the forgiveness Jesus secured is in a different league. The Bible sees sin as a debt owed by the sinner to God, yet entirely at his initiative, those in whose place Jesus died receive 'forgiveness of sins through his name'(Acts 10:43). In the death of Jesus, Christians are released from the double burden of guilt and debt and are freely and fully forgiven—for ever: 'There is therefore now no condemnation for those who are in Christ Jesus' (Romans 8:1).

God accepts the death of Christ as the full and complete payment of every penalty that his holy law requires and which assures the full and free pardon of all of a Christian's sins, *past, present and future.* This does not mean that a Christian is perfect, with no need for daily forgiveness and cleansing, and we will look at this in a later chapter. The all-important thing to realize at this point is that justification is full, perfect, complete and final, bringing the Christian into a position from which they can never be removed.

Finally, there is *reconciliation.* This means bringing back together those who have been separated for one reason or another. By nature and choice we are all separated from God because of our self-centred rebellion against his authority and our determination to go our own way. As Jesus puts it, 'The light has come into the world, and people loved the darkness rather than the light because their deeds were evil' (John 3:19). The Bible goes even further and says that because of sin God has become man's enemy: 'For the wrath of God is revealed from heaven against all ungodliness and unrighteousness of men' (Romans 1:18).

Yet God (the innocent party) has taken the initiative and done something astonishing to enable man (the guilty party) to be at peace with him by dealing with the root cause of the rift—human sin. In the death of his Son, God not only punished human sin but also satisfied his own justice, and in this way removed the barrier separating him from sinners. This is why the apostle Paul writes, 'While we were enemies we were reconciled to God by the death of his Son' (Romans 5:10) and tells Christians, 'You who once were far off have been brought near by the blood of Christ' (Ephesians 2:13).

Elsewhere he writes, 'Therefore, since we have been justified by faith, we have peace with God through our Lord Jesus Christ' (Romans 5:1). Once in rebellion against God, Christians now stand in a totally different relationship to him. Unbelievers are God's enemies; Christians are his friends, because the death of Christ has put away the one thing—sin—that kept them apart.

At the precise moment Jesus died, God provided an amazing visual aid to illustrate this. In the temple in Jerusalem, the focal point of Israel's worship, a richly-embroidered veil or curtain separated the Holy Place from the Most Holy Place, the inner sanctuary that represented God's presence. As Jesus drew his last breath, 'The curtain of the temple was torn in two, from top to bottom' (Matthew 27:51). This miracle was a sign that whereas under the old religious system only the high priest could enter the symbolic presence of God, and then only once a year, the death of Jesus removed for ever the sin barrier between God and man, so that all those for whom he died could be reconciled to God without any religious trappings. This is why Christians have 'confidence to enter the holy places by the blood of Jesus, by the new and living way that he opened for us through the curtain, that is, through his flesh' (Hebrews 10:19).

One of the Psalms begins with the words, 'It is good to give thanks to the LORD' (Psalm 92:1)—and it is. It prevents us being self-centred, and gives God the glory he deserves. Take a few moments to reflect on what you have just read in the last two chapters (you might even want to read them again). As a Christian, you have been justified (made right with God), ransomed from captivity to sin, freely and completely forgiven and reconciled to your Creator. David begins one of his Psalms by declaring, 'I will bless the LORD at all times; his praise shall continually be in my mouth', and adds, 'Oh magnify the LORD with me, and let us exalt his name together' (Psalm 34:1,3). As a Christian, you have every reason to do so!

A NEW FAMILY

It can be said of Christians that 'the people dwelling in darkness have seen a great light' (Matthew 4:16), and in the last two chapters we have seen some of its brilliance. Before showing how believers can be sure these things are true for them, we need to see another shaft of light the Bible shines on what it means to be a Christian.

After he had created Adam, God said, 'It is not good that the man should be alone' (Genesis 2:18), so he created a woman (Adam later called her Eve) with whom Adam could share his life. In doing this, God brought the first human family into being, and ever since then secure and harmonious family life has been one of God's greatest blessings. This is matched by the fact that everyone who becomes a Christian is immediately adopted into 'the family of believers' (Galatians 6:10), a family in which there are no distinctions of age, colour, education or social standing, but where the members are 'all one [*that is, equal*] in Christ Jesus' (Galatians 3:28).

God's adoption of Christians into his family may be the Cinderella of New Testament doctrine (given much less attention than it deserves), but it is hugely important. It is not mentioned in the Old Testament, as adoption was not part of Jewish culture. This helps us to understand why the apostle Paul (the only New Testament writer who uses the word 'adoption') wrote about it only in letters to areas under Roman rule (Galatia, Ephesus and Rome). As the Roman legal system made provision for adoption, Paul's readers would more easily grasp what he was saying.

In Chapter 3 we saw that justification explains Christians' relationship to God's law. Adoption goes further and declares that Christians are members of God's family, with all the rights and privileges involved. This gives us an even fuller understanding of what it means to be a Christian. As Sinclair Ferguson says, 'The fact that a judge pronounces the verdict of 'not guilty' does not commit him to take the accused home and allow him all the privileges of his son!' Yet this is what God does. All those who are justified through faith in Christ are given the status of sons and daughters of God. Adoption places a person in the position where they have the 'legal' rights of a son; the very word 'adoption' literally means 'the placing of a son'. Adoption does not change a Christian's character, but it does change their relationship to God, their standing, their rights and their privileges. Paul writes about adoption in three tenses, and what it means will become clearer as we look at these in order.

PAST, PRESENT AND FUTURE

Firstly, Paul writes about adoption in the *past tense:* '[*God*] chose us in [*Christ*] before the foundation of the world, that we should be holy and blameless before him. In love he predestined us for adoption through Jesus Christ, according to the purpose of his will, to the praise of his glorious grace, with which he has blessed us in the Beloved' (Ephesians 1:4-6). This points us to the doctrine of election, the truth that before time began God chose out a people for himself. Christians are not members of God's family because they chose God to be their Father, but because God chose them—and that choice was made not only before they were born, but before the cosmos was created. This amazing truth, which the British author Peter Jeffery calls 'one of the most thrilling and humbling truths in Scripture' is impossible to understand, but vitally important to accept. Becoming a Christian is not something we choose, or to which we contribute—how could we do either before we were born?

Secondly, Paul writes about adoption in the *present tense*. He tells Christians at Rome, 'You have received the Spirit of adoption as sons' (Romans 8:15). The Holy Spirit not only enables us to repent and put our trust in Christ, he also assures us that we are members of God's family. The apostle John underlines this: 'See what kind of love the Father has given to us, that we should be called children of God; and so we are', then adds, 'Beloved, we are God's children *now*' (1 John 3: 1-2).

Thirdly, Paul writes about adoption in the *future tense*. He says that 'we wait eagerly for our adoption as sons, the redemption of our bodies' (Romans 8:23). This looks forward to the moment when the purpose of our adoption will be complete and the whole universe will see that Christians truly are the sons of God. Paul adds to this by saying that Christians are 'heirs of God and fellow heirs with Christ' (Romans 8:17). The heir to a throne may go almost unnoticed in a photograph of a Royal Family, but when the moment comes for him to be crowned, the whole world recognizes him. Paul says that in the life to come there will be no doubt that Christians have been adopted into God's eternal family.

This chapter has concentrated on the privileged status of Christians as children of God, but it will be helpful to add one other thing. One New Testament writer quotes the Old Testament saying, 'My son, do not regard lightly the discipline of the Lord, nor be weary when reproved by him. For the Lord disciplines the one he loves, and chastises every son whom he receives' then adds, 'It is for discipline that you have to endure. God is treating you as sons. For what son is there whom his father does not discipline?' (Hebrews 12:5-7). The word 'discipline' means 'training' and when a father properly disciplines a child it is an act of love, an action deliberately calculated to be for the child's good. In the Christian life, God sometimes causes or allows his children to endure hardship or suffering, but it is always intended to result in his glory and their blessing. The more a Christian grows in grace, the more they will come to see that even the hard things in life are under God's control, and the more they will be willing to praise the Lord for the discipline that trains them towards Christian maturity and prepares them for their ultimate destiny in glory.

6

CAN YOU BE SURE?

IT HAS SOMETIMES BEEN SAID that nothing in the world causes so much misery as uncertainty, and it is not difficult to agree. Family matters, personal relationships, health, finance, moving house or employment issues—all can produce the misery that comes with uncertainty. The same can be true of spiritual issues, and for the professing Christian uncertainty can arise over the most fundamental of all: 'I am putting my trust in Jesus Christ, but sometimes I wonder whether my sins are really forgiven and whether I can be sure of going to heaven when I die. There are times when I even doubt God's loving interest in me.'

Does this ring a bell? If it does, you are not unique. Countless believers have times when they wrestle with the same uncertainties, and may even go through weeks or months when they have lost their assurance of salvation and even doubt God's presence and love. Israel's King David is one of the most remarkable Old Testament believers. He was not only an outstanding ruler, military commander, statesman and musician, God also called him 'a man after my heart' (Acts 13:22). Yet David's life had deep valleys as well as great mountain tops, and at one point he even cried out, 'My God, my God, why have you forsaken me? Why are you so far from saving me?' (Psalm 22:1). It is difficult to imagine getting any lower than that, yet among his last recorded words were these: 'The LORD lives, and blessed be my rock, and exalted be my God, the rock of my salvation' (2 Samuel 22:47). David's despair was an episode, not an indication that he had lost his salvation, and the idea that Christians go through life on an uninterrupted spiritual and emotional 'high', with never a moment of doubt, is fantasy, not fact.

On the other hand, the doctrine of assurance runs like a golden thread throughout the New Testament. The apostle John says that the very reason he wrote his first letter to the Christians of his day was 'that you may *know* that you have eternal life' (1 John 5:13). The Bible tells us that we can and should be sure of this.

THE SAVIOUR'S WORK

The first important thing to realize about assurance is that it is objective rather than subjective. In other words, it is not based on our feelings, hopes or longings, but on certainties outside of ourselves. Take someone who says, 'I am putting my trust in Jesus Christ, but how can I know that my sins are forgiven and that God will never hold me accountable for them?' The answer to that question is this: *because Jesus is alive!*

Many years ago in England, people owing money could be sent to what were known as 'debtors' prisons' until the debt was paid. If the debtor ran away and could not be traced, their guarantor (someone who had agreed to pay the debt if the debtor failed to do so) would be sent to prison in his place. Now imagine that you had run away in serious debt and that your guarantor had been jailed in your place.

Some time later, you returned to your home town and saw your guarantor walking down the road, a free man. That would tell you that he had paid your debt, that all the demands of justice had been met and that you too were free. Your assurance would not be based on your hopes or feelings, but on the fact that the one who took responsibility for your debt had been released from prison. Now grasp this: your assurance of salvation rests on the fact that the Lord Jesus Christ, who paid the death penalty for your sin, was raised to life and freed from death's prison. This is why the apostle Paul can assure Christians that God has 'forgiven us all our trespasses, by cancelling the record of debt that stood against us with its legal demands. This he set aside, nailing it to the cross' (Colossians 2:13-14).

Elsewhere, he puts it even more concisely, saying that Jesus 'was delivered up for our trespasses and raised for our justification' (Romans 4:25). In this statement the word 'for' means 'on account of' or 'because of'. This tells us that Jesus' resurrection was proof that he had paid once for all and in full the penalty for his people's sins. God will not condemn those for whom Jesus has already paid sin's death penalty— and nobody else can. As Paul puts it: 'Who shall bring any charge against God's elect? It is God who justifies. Who is to condemn? Christ Jesus is the one who died—more than that, who was raised— who is at the right hand of God, who indeed is interceding for us' (Romans 8:33-34). The evidence for the resurrection of Jesus is overwhelming (I have written about this in *Jesus: Dead or Alive?* –published by EP Books) and all who put their trust in him can be sure that they are free for ever from sin's guilt and condemnation.

THE FATHER'S WORD

The second important fact on which Christians can base their assurance of salvation is that God keeps his word—'It is impossible for God to lie' (Hebrews 6:18). The Bible teems with promises God makes to believers, and one of the greatest is that those who truly put their trust in Jesus Christ can never lose their salvation. Jesus himself makes this crystal clear: 'Truly, truly, I say to you, whoever hears my word and believes him who sent me *has* eternal life. He *does not* come into judgment, but *has* passed from death to life' (John 5:24).

In 1798, a band of armed men terrorized County Wexford in Ireland, plundering homes and murdering local farmers. The viceroy, Lord Cornwallis, was determined to turn these outlaws into useful, law-abiding citizens, so he made them an amazing offer. He bought a certain field and promised that any rebel, whatever his record might be, who stepped into that field and laid down his weapons would receive a full pardon. At first, the rebels did not believe it; it must be a trap. Finally, one of the worst members of the gang decided to risk his life on the promise being true. He walked into the field, threw down his weapons and waited to see what happened. A few minutes later a soldier appeared, asked the man his name, wrote it on a piece of paper and handed the document to him. When he looked at it, the rebel saw that it was an official act of pardon signed by Lord Cornwallis. He was a free man the moment he entered that field; he was sure of this when he saw Lord Cornwallis' signature on a pardon bearing his own name. Eventually many other rebels followed his example and the whole area was transformed as a result. If anyone had later threatened them with arrest, they had only to produce their signed pardons and no charge could ever be brought against them.

In a much more wonderful way, the Christian is saved by trusting Christ and he can be sure by knowing and trusting the great promises of salvation contained in the Bible, as these bear God's signature. Paul gives us one of the greatest: 'For I am sure that neither death nor life, nor angels nor rulers, nor things present nor things to come, nor powers, nor height nor depth, nor anything else in all creation, will be able to separate us from the love of God in Christ Jesus our Lord' (Romans 8:38-39).

THE SPIRIT'S WITNESS

The third important fact is the witness of the Holy Spirit. We will look more closely at the Holy Spirit's person and work in Chapter 14, but concentrate here on the way he assures Christians of their salvation. Paul tells Christians at Rome, 'For you did not receive the spirit of slavery to fall back into fear, but you have received the Spirit of adoption as sons, by whom we cry, "Abba! Father!" The Spirit himself bears witness with our spirit that we are children of God' (Romans 8:15-16). The Holy Spirit not only places Christians into God's family but indwells them from that moment onwards. Every Christian without exception has received the Holy Spirit; as the Bible makes clear, 'Anyone who does not have the Spirit of Christ does not belong to him' (Romans 8: 9).

When Paul says we can call God 'Abba! Father!' he is telling us of one specific result of the Holy Spirit's presence in a believer's heart. The word 'Abba' is not Greek (the New Testament language) but Aramaic, which was widely used in the Middle East at that time. It was an intimate, familiar word that would be used by a child in speaking informally to its father. The only other time it is used in the New Testament is when Jesus, under tremendous pressure just before his crucifixion, cries out, 'Abba, Father, all things are possible for you' (Mark 14:36). Because of the presence of the Holy Spirit in their hearts, Christians can call God by the same intimate name Jesus used then.

Whenever you are warmly conscious (perhaps when praying) of an intimate relationship with your heavenly Father, this is the work of the Holy Spirit confirming that you truly are a child of God. When in praying you sense God's presence, know that you truly love him and that he loves you, and find your heart going out to him in praise, thanksgiving and joy, these convictions (they are much deeper than mere feelings) are the result of the Holy Spirit's work within you. When you truly worship God, you are not following a mechanical formula or a religious routine. Instead, you are enjoying one of the great privileges of your relationship with your heavenly Father. Even as you worship, the Holy Spirit assures you that the relationship is real.

THE BELIEVER'S WALK

The fourth important piece of evidence on which believers can base their assurance is their gradual growth towards Christian maturity. The Bible says, 'If anyone is in Christ he is a new creation. The old has passed away; behold, the new has come' (2 Corinthians 5:17). This does not mean that a person who becomes a Christian suddenly becomes perfect (more about that in a later chapter), but that just as human parents can expect physical development in their children, so there will always be lifestyle changes in a true believer. Our beliefs should be matched by our behaviour, and the Bible warns us that when this is not the case a person's claim to be a Christian is false. As one New Testament writer bluntly puts it, 'For as the body apart from the spirit is dead, so also faith apart from works is dead' (James 2:26).

No Bible writer links belief and behaviour more clearly

than the apostle John. Here are some of the things he writes, with the behaviour element emphasized: 'And by this we know that we have come to know [*God*] *if we keep his commandments.* Whoever says, "I know him" *but does not keep his commandments* is a liar, and the truth is not in him' (1 John 2:3-4). 'We know that we have passed out of death into life, *because we love the brothers*'(1 John 3:14). 'Little children, let us not love in word or talk, *but in deed and in truth.* By this we shall know that we are of the truth, and reassure our heart before him' (1 John 3 18-19).

These statements make it clear that anyone who claims to be a Christian, but whose behaviour is not being changed is deceiving themselves. Now apply the test to yourself! Are you honestly and earnestly seeking to be obedient to God's revealed will? (more about this in Chapter 15). Are you steadily making spiritual progress? Are you gradually overcoming old sinful habits? Do you long to become more and more like Jesus in your thoughts, words and actions? Paul writes to the Christians at Corinth, 'Examine yourselves, to see whether you are in the faith. Test yourselves' (2 Corinthians 13:5). Doing this is an important way of checking whether your assurance has a firm basis.

7

GOD'S HOUSEHOLD

IN CHAPTER 5 we saw the amazing truth that at the moment of their conversion Christians are adopted into God's 'family of believers' (Galatians 6:10), a family in which there are no distinctions of age, colour, education or social standing. The Bible also calls this 'the household of God' (Ephesians 2:19), but this is not a vague term with no visible expression. Instead, God expects his family members to be clearly identifiable here on earth, and the most familiar name for this is 'the church'. People often use the word 'church' to mean religion in general, or a profession (people training to 'go into the church'), or special buildings, but although the word occurs about 170 times in the Bible, it is never used in any one of these three ways.

In the New Testament, the original Greek word for 'church' is *ekklesia*, which basically means a gathering of people. It was not necessarily a religious word, and was also used to describe a democratic meeting of citizens to carry out lawful civic affairs. For instance, when Paul's preaching causes a tremendous stir in the city of Ephesus, the town clerk tells the people that any complaints against the apostle will have to be dealt with 'in the regular assembly (*ekklesia*)' (Acts 19:39)

Used in a Christian context the church is a family of people God has gathered from all over the world and who belong to him. That said, the Bible does use building metaphors to describe it. Paul tells the Christians at Corinth, 'You are... God's building' (1 Corinthians 3:9) and Peter tells the Christians to whom he writes: 'As you come to [*Christ*], a living stone rejected by men but in the sight of God chosen and precious, you yourselves like living stones are being built up as a spiritual house' (1 Peter 2:4-5). The Christian church is not a pile of bricks and mortar, but is made up of living stones, people cemented by faith in the Lord Jesus Christ, the corner-stone who holds the whole building together.

THE 3-D CHURCH

The Christian church is vastly bigger than people think, as it is made up of all God's people since the beginning of time, and we can therefore think of it in three ways.

To begin with the overall picture, the church 'building' will not be completed until the end of time, after Jesus returns to the earth in great glory (more on this in Chapter 17) and it will by then be 'a great multitude that no one could number, from every nation, from all tribes and peoples and languages' (Revelation 7:9). This will be an amazing fulfilment of the promise God made to the Old Testament patriarch Abram when he came to faith: 'Look towards heaven, and number the stars, if you are able to number them... So shall your offspring be' (Genesis 15:5). God later changed Abram's name to Abraham, which means 'father of a multitude', and one day, in great glory, God will fulfil the promise he made to him.

Secondly, part of this vast assembly is today's global church, made up of Christians all over the world, worshipping and serving God in many different ways and places, all belonging to 'the family of believers' (Galatians 6:10).

The third aspect is that of the local church, groups of like-minded believers who meet regularly to worship and serve God. This is not the place to explain why there are so many different denominations and groupings of so called Christian churches, but most came into being because people felt the need to emphasize particular aspects of Christian doctrine or practice, or to protest against current trends in their church at that time. Yet we must never lose sight of the fact that the true church, what Paul calls 'the church of the living God' (1 Timothy 3:15), is *one,* and can never be divided. As he tells the Ephesians 'There is one body and one Spirit—just as you were called to the one hope that belongs to your call—one Lord, one faith, one baptism, one God and Father of all, who is over all and through all and in all' (Ephesians 4: 4-6).

However, there is one fundamental difference between the present 'visible' church here on earth and the complete church to come. The present church is flawed, whereas at the end of time the church will be 'without spot or wrinkle or any such thing…holy and without blemish' (Ephesians 5:27). Many who attend local churches have some kind of faith, but do not have a personal relationship with Jesus, so are not truly in God's family. They may even make a sincere contribution to the running and finances of the local church as an organization, but this in itself is no true mark of saving faith, nor is baptism, confirmation, church membership or the holding of any ecclesiastical office.

Sadly, there are many who attend church on Sunday, but for the rest of the week give little or no sign of having been

born again. This was true even in the early days of the
Christian church. In Samaria, a magician by the name of
Simon was baptized and identified himself with the local,
visible church, but when he offered to buy his way into a
position of spiritual power Peter told him, 'May your silver
perish with you, because you thought you could obtain the
gift of God with money!... your heart is not right before
God... you are in the gall of bitterness and in the bond of
iniquity' (Acts 8:20-23). For a brief time at least, Simon was
a member of the local church, and people no doubt thought
he was a Christian, but he had never been truly born again.

THE NEW TESTAMENT WAY

As we have seen, the future church will be perfect. In the
meantime, there are biblical principles and practices that
should mark the local church today.

Firstly, *worship that gives glory to God*. The New
Testament church was marked by 'praising God' (Acts 2:47),
and this is a distinguishing mark of any true church. In one
of his great hymns of praise, Paul cries, 'To [*God*] be glory
in the church and in Christ Jesus throughout all
generations, for ever and ever. Amen' (Ephesians 3:21).
There is something seriously wrong whenever the emphasis
in a local church is on the building, the music, the form of
service, or even on the personality or performance of its
leader. Those attending a local church should do so in the
spirit of the psalmist, who cries out, 'Let us come into his
presence with thanksgiving; let us make a joyful noise to
him with songs of praise!... Oh come, let us worship and
bow down; let us kneel before the LORD, our Maker! For
he is our God, and we are the people of his pasture, and the
sheep of his hand' (Psalm 95:2, 6-7). There should be no
place for frivolous, shallow and man-centred 'worship' that

aims at pleasing the congregation rather than our awesome God.

Secondly, *sound doctrine.* Those early Christians 'devoted themselves to the apostles' teaching' (Acts 2:42). New converts were not expected to learn about the Christian faith by meeting in discussion groups, with one person's opinion carrying as much weight as the next. Instead, they gladly submitted to the God-given ministry of the apostles. Today, discussion groups have their place, but should never replace the authoritative teaching of God's Word by those called and equipped to give it. The Bible says, 'Do not be led away by diverse and strange teachings' (Hebrews 13:9), and the surest way to avoid error is to grow in the knowledge of the truth. A church being true to New Testament principles will be marked by the consistent, diligent preaching of the Word of God.

Thirdly, *united prayer.* Another mark of the early church was their devotion to 'prayers' (Acts 2:42). It was when 'many were gathered together and were praying' (Acts 12:12) that God worked in a miraculous way to release Peter from the pagan ruler Herod's prison. God still works in many ways today in response to the united prayers of his people, and a regular prayer meeting is important in the life of a local church.

Fourthly, *the right administration of the sacraments.* There are two New Testament sacraments binding on the Christian church. One is the baptism of believers, and the other is the Breaking of Bread (otherwise known as The Lord's Supper or Holy Communion). Early believers 'were baptized' (Acts 2:41) and 'devoted themselves to... the breaking of bread' (Acts 2:42). Both sacraments were instituted by Jesus himself, as 'the head of the church' (Ephesians 5:23). In sending the first disciples out on their world-wide mission he tells them that they are to 'make disciples of all nations, baptizing them in the name of the Father and of the Son and of the Holy Spirit' (Matthew 28:19), and after sharing the bread and wine at his last evening meal with them, he adds, 'Do this in remembrance of me' (1 Corinthians 11:24-25).

Baptism is an outward symbol of repentance and faith, a sign to the world that the person baptized professes to trust Jesus as Saviour and acknowledges him as Lord. The breaking of bread is a symbolic meal in which Christians gratefully remind themselves that their fellowship with God and with each other is based entirely on Christ's death on their behalf. As Paul tells the Corinthians, 'For as often as you eat this bread and drink the cup, you proclaim the Lord's death until he comes' (1 Corinthians 11:26). Any local church seeking to base its practice on the New Testament will include both of these sacraments, and individual Christians seeking to be obedient to the Bible's teaching will gladly receive them.

Fifthly, *warm-hearted fellowship*. One of the greatest descriptions of the church in the whole Bible is that it is 'the body of Christ' (1 Corinthians 12:27), a statement which underlines its spiritual life and unity. Paul elaborates: 'For as in one body we have many members, and the members do not all have the same function, so we, though many, are one body in Christ, and individually members one of another' (Romans 12:4-5). A local church is meant to be much more than what someone has called 'a loose association of Jesus's Facebook friends'. In the deepest possible sense, Christians belong to each other; they are joined together in the common life they draw from Jesus, and they are meant to show it by the sharing of that common life with other believers. A human body only functions healthily when there is unrestricted circulation of life-giving blood, and the church only functions healthily when its members freely share their spiritual lives with each other. This will have a practical outcome, as members do all they can to meet the needs of others. Nobody within a local church fellowship should suffer from a need that can and should be met, and the church should also be reaching out to help in meeting needs in its local community. As John puts it, 'Let us not love in word or talk but in deed and in truth (1 John 3:18).

Sixthly, *continuous evangelism.* We read of the early church that 'the Lord added to their number day by day those who were being saved' (Acts 2:47) and as 'faith comes from hearing, and hearing through the word of Christ' (Romans 10:17) this obviously means that the church was continuously engaged in evangelism, as every local church should be. Not every service or meeting held in a church will be specifically aimed at unbelievers, but throughout its activities among children, young people, the elderly and other groups in its local community the straightforward message of the gospel will come through loud and clear. People will be faced with the fact of their sin, the danger of their condition, the love of God, the death and resurrection of Christ, the need for conversion, the brevity of life, the certainty of death and the reality of judgement. Nor should a local church's concern be limited to its own locality or country. Its vision should be world-wide and it will do all it can to support the work of overseas missionary enterprise, sharing in the tremendous task of taking the gospel 'to the end of the earth' (Acts 1:8).

❧ 8 ❧

BE THERE!

IN THE LAST chapter we saw what a local church should look like if it is based on New Testament principles; in this chapter we will see why you should be involved in one. We are told that Jesus "as was his custom... went to the synagogue on the Sabbath day' (Luke 4:16), and after his resurrection his disciples met together 'on the first day of the week' (Acts 20:7) to worship God. Today, the Bible's instructions are clear: 'Let us consider how to stir up one another to love and good works, *not neglecting to meet together,* as is the habit of some, but encouraging one another, and all the more as you see the Day approaching' (Hebrews 10:23-25). The words 'the Day' mean the day when Jesus returns, and as that day is now some 2,000 years nearer than when these instructions were first written they are more immediately relevant now than they have ever been.

Membership of a local church is not to be an optional extra for Christians. It is a Bible-based duty. Ideally, your choice of a local church will be one whose beliefs and activities are true to God's Word. If you are a new Christian you may need to ask advice, perhaps from the person who told you about Jesus and guided you towards becoming a Christian, but do not hold back from joining a church because it seems to have weaknesses in one of the areas we looked at. No church is perfect, but there is no way in which it can ever be improved by true Christians staying away from it. Here are some of the reasons why you should be there.

Because it shows that you love the Lord Jesus Christ, who makes the great promise that 'where two or three are gathered in my name, there am I among them' (Matthew 18:20). When someone you love promises to be somewhere at a certain time, would you deliberately choose not to be there? The Christian life consists of relationships with Christ and other believers and we should do all we can to deepen these. One of the Psalmists cries, 'O God... a day in your courts is better than a thousand elsewhere' (Psalm 84:9-10), and another says, 'Sing to the LORD a new song, his praise in the assembly of the godly!' (Psalm 149:1). Be sure to join them; Christian faith is intensely personal, but it is never meant to be private.

Because the church is unique. People can sometimes feel irritated or uncomfortable in church because of noisy children, poor singing, music that is too loud, hymns that are too modern (or too ancient), preaching that is too long (or too short), or by any one of a long list of other things. Yet no other gathering of people comes close to the special place that the local church has in God's eyes. The Bible says, 'For the LORD takes delight in his people' (Psalm 149:4). If the Lord takes pleasure in the company of his people, you should aim to do the same.

Because gathering with God's people is one way of giving thanks to God for his goodness to you. In the fourth of the Ten Commandments God says of one day in seven that we are to 'keep it holy' (Exodus 20:8). The root meaning of 'holy' tells us that one day in seven is to be *different*. In his great kindness God has ordained one day a week (sometimes called 'the Lord's Day') in which we can lay aside the pressures of daily life and recharge our physical and spiritual batteries. For two thousand years the church has seen this special day, Sunday, as a precious gift from God, enabling Christians not only to rest from daily chores but to benefit from all the blessings that flow from true worship and genuine fellowship —and to thank God for them.

Because every Christian thrives on encouragement. Encouragement has been called 'oxygen for the soul' and we all know what a boost it gives us. The need for encouragement is so important that the writer of Hebrews says, 'Exhort one another every day, as long as it is called "today", that none of you may be hardened by the deceitfulness of sin' (Hebrews 3:13). It is difficult to exaggerate the importance of Christians encouraging one another as they battle against the pressures of a secular society. There is so much going on (and going wrong) in the world today that Christians who are prepared to get alongside other believers, helping, guiding, comforting, strengthening or sympathizing with them have a vital part to play. Not only are Christians 'members of [*Christ's*] body' (Ephesians 5:30) they are also 'members one of another' (Ephesians 4:25) and that unity is dynamically demonstrated when they meet together. Even if you feel that (at least for the time being) there is not much you can contribute, just being there will be an encouragement both to you and to others, not least to the pastor or church leader as he dedicates his life to serving other believers.

Because you should make every possible use of the means of grace that God provides. Within the fellowship of the church the preaching and teaching of the Bible, the sacraments of baptism and the Lord's Supper, praise, prayer and fellowship with other believers are the most important means of grace for God's people, and Christians need all of them. No Christians know the Bible so well, are so well grounded in doctrine, and are so well equipped to counter a secular culture that they have no need for well-prepared teaching by a man set apart to 'shepherd the flock of God' (1 Peter 5:2). No Christians are so far advanced in holiness and pray so adequately at home that they have no need of the means of grace that God provides in a gathering of his people. Meeting with other Christians will help you to 'grow in the grace and knowledge of our Lord and Saviour Jesus Christ' (2 Peter 3:18).

Because it says something significant to an unbelieving world. When your neighbours see you going regularly to church, or your friends, school, student or work colleagues or others know that you do, you will be bearing witness to the fact that you have found something more important than any other activities or pleasures. If you have family members who are not Christians, your behaviour at home and in their company and elsewhere should underline the significance of your faith and your church attendance. Jesus said, 'Whoever does not gather with me scatters' (Matthew 12:30). Make sure that your daily life endorses the message other people get by seeing how you use the Lord's Day. Above all, aim to live in such a way as to 'make the teaching about God our Saviour attractive' (Titus 2:10, NIV).

9

KEEPING IN TOUCH (1)

HUMAN RELATIONSHIPS ARE DEVELOPED by people keeping in touch with each other, and nothing is more important to Christians than keeping in close touch with God, their heavenly Father. In the next two chapters we will see something of what this means. In this chapter we will focus on God speaking to us.

The most direct way in which he does this is through the Bible, 'the living and abiding word of God' (1 Peter 1:23). The Bible is a collection of sixty-six books written by about forty human authors over a period of some 1,500 years. It includes law, history, poetry, prophecy and many other ways of expressing truth. The Bible is without error, as all the authors were inspired by God, though it reflects the human style of each author. It is divided into two parts, the Old and New Testaments. A testament (or covenant) is a binding agreement, and these two reveal God's plan to bring men and women into a right relationship with himself. There is about 400 years between the testaments, but their theme is the same. They are like two halves of one amazing story that reveals the attributes and character of God, the nature of man, and the way in which their broken relationship can be restored.

It is interesting to see how often God's Word is compared to food. One psalm says, 'How sweet are your words to my taste, sweeter than honey to my mouth!' (Psalm 119:103) and the prophet Jeremiah tells God, 'Your words were found, and I ate them; and your words became to me a joy and the delight of my heart' (Jeremiah 15:16). What food is to physical life, the Bible is to spiritual life, and this helps us to learn a number of simple but important lessons.

REGULAR MEALS

Anyone who neglects to eat properly endangers their physical health, and the person who neglects feeding on the Word of God is bound to suffer spiritually. In the physical world, the main results of diet deficiency are lack of appetite, stunted growth, deformed features and susceptibility to disease, and every one of these has a spiritual parallel.

Lack of appetite? In a tragic way, lack of Bible intake leads to lack of Bible desire. Do everything you can to avoid this vicious circle. Instead, try to follow the Old Testament example of Job, who was able to say, 'I have treasured the words of [*God's*] mouth more than my portion of food' (Job 23:12).

Stunted growth? When Paul ends a visit to the church at Ephesus he tells the elders, 'I commend you to God and to the word of his grace, which is able to build you up' (Acts 20:32). Christians who neglect the Bible soon lose spiritual strength and fail to grow. Deformed features? Good, regular food makes a vital contribution to good health, which shows in the shape and tone of the body and the texture of the skin. Disciplined feeding on God's Word shows in a healthy and attractive spiritual life. As one of the psalmists tells God, 'I have stored up your word in my heart, that I might not sin against you' (Psalm 119:11). Susceptibility to disease? Jesus tells certain religious leaders that they get into all kinds of trouble because, 'you know neither the Scriptures nor the power of God' (Mark 12:24). As a Christian, you will face countless theological and practical questions in life, and if you neglect your Bible you will find it impossible to answer them wisely and well. As the psalmist tells God, 'Your word is a lamp to my feet and a light to my path' (Psalm 119:105).

Are you feeding regularly on God's Word? Is your intake sufficient to keep you spiritually healthy? If you are going without at least one meal a day you are living dangerously! Having said that, Christians must not get locked into the precise time of day when they should read their Bibles, or how long they should spend in Bible study every day, any more than they should be legalistic about sitting down to eat at exactly the same time every day, or taking the same number of minutes over each meal. A person's age, daily schedule, family and other responsibilities, spiritual maturity, and ability to study closely will all play a part here. The all-important thing is not that your Bible study is regimented, but that it is regular and sufficient to keep you well nourished.

A BALANCED DIET

We know that vitamins, proteins, carbohydrates, minerals and other elements each play an important part in maintaining physical health and strength, and that an unbalanced diet can cause as much damage as an insufficient one. Boiled potatoes may be fine, but boiled potatoes alone three times a day would not be ideal! In spiritual eating, the same principles hold good. The Bible is not only unequalled in value as spiritual food, but also in the perfectly balanced variety of its content. Its human authors came from different countries, lived at different times, spoke different languages and expressed themselves in different ways, but they all 'spoke from God as they were carried along by the Holy Spirit' (2 Peter 1:21).

The result is a larder full of fascinating food; make sure you make the most of it! Beware of reading only the New Testament and ignoring the Old, or vice-versa. Never stay too long in any one part of the Bible, and never make the mistake of reading only those parts of the Bible that appeal to you. Remember that '*all Scripture* is breathed out by God and profitable for teaching, for reproof, for correction, and for training in righteousness, that the man of God may be competent, equipped for every good work' (2 Timothy 3:16-17). A friend of mine was once the thinnest boy in his class at school, but later became the holder of a number of national weightlifting records. He told me that one of the secrets of his success was that he began to eat wisely and well, carefully ensuring that his diet included all those things calculated to strengthen his body. The lesson for Christians is obvious.

THE IMPORTANCE OF DIGESTION

In the physical world we have become increasingly aware of the value of careful digestion. The spiritual parallel is the danger of hurriedly glancing at a Bible passage and then dashing off to do something else. We need to read the Bible straightforwardly to get the facts, study it seriously to get the meaning and think about it seriously and carefully to get the benefit. Use a good, sound, modern version of the Bible—ask advice to make sure you buy a good accurate translation and not a paraphrase. If you are unsure which one to use, ask for advice from mature Christians who study the Bible regularly. As soon as possible, choose one version and use this for your main reading and study; chopping and changing from one to another will only confuse you, and make it more difficult to find, mark or memorize key verses.

You will benefit from using one of the many Bible Reading Notes available today; ask your church leader or other Christian friends for help about these. There is no space here to list or assess them, but in *How to enjoy your Bible*, published by EP Books, I have gone into great detail about Daily Notes, Study Bibles, commentaries and electronic aids to Bible study, as well as showing eight ways to explore what the Bible has to say, so you may find a copy of that book helpful. Whatever your approach, trust God's promise to his early disciples that the Holy Spirit will 'guide you into all the truth' (John 16:13). Come to your Bible with the psalmist's prayer, 'Open my eyes, that I may behold wondrous things out of your law' (Psalm 119:18). As you focus your mind on a passage, ask yourself whether there is a truth for you to learn, a promise for you to claim, a commandment for you to obey, a warning for you to heed, a challenge for you to face, or action for you to take. Allow God's Word to get into your spiritual bloodstream so that it will find expression in your daily behavior.

Come to the Bible regularly, because there is not a day in your life when it is not relevant. Come to it gratefully, remembering that it is part of God's gracious provision for you. Come to it diligently, accepting that genuine Bible study will mean discipline and effort. Come to it prayerfully, asking for God's help in understanding its true meaning. Come to it submissively, accepting its absolute authority in every part of your life. As the seventeenth-century preacher Thomas Watson put it, 'Think in every line you read that God is speaking to you.' I can think of no better advice to give you!

BEYOND THE PAGE TO THE PERSON

There is no need to know personally the people who grew, harvested, packed, prepared or delivered our food. But as we 'feed' on the Bible, developing a relationship with its heavenly Author is essential. Speaking to critics who refused to believe his claim to be divine, Jesus tells them, 'You search the Scriptures because you think that in them you have eternal life; and it is they that bear witness about me, yet you refuse to come to me that you may have life' (John 5:39-40). They were diligent Old Testament readers, but they failed to see that it pointed to Jesus. As you come to the Bible, determine above everything else that you are going to get *beyond the page to the person*. Never be satisfied with merely gaining knowledge, storing information, analyzing truth, memorizing favourite verses or remembering facts. *The Word of God is meant to lead you to the God of the Word;* as it does, you will treasure the time you spend in it.

10

KEEPING IN TOUCH (2)

As God speaks to us directly through his written word, so we can speak directly to him through prayer, which deepens our communion with him. Prayer is not meant to be a shopping-list, but a God-given means of developing a two-way relationship.

One mistake people sometimes make is to think that they can only pray when they feel 'ready' to. They may feel unprepared, or out of touch, or spiritually below par, so decide to give prayer a miss until they feel in a better frame of mind. Yet as we saw in Chapter 4, the curtain of the temple in Jerusalem being supernaturally torn in two the moment Jesus died was a God-given visual aid, telling us that the 'door' of direct prayer was now open. Sharing this great truth some time later, the writer of Hebrews says, 'Therefore, brothers, since *we have confidence to enter the holy places* by the blood of Jesus, by the new and living way that he opened for us through the curtain, that is, through his flesh, and since we have a great priest over the house of God, *let us draw near with a true heart in full assurance of faith*' (Hebrews 10:19-22).

Notice the words I have deliberately emphasized. The Bible says that Christians can approach God with confidence, and with full assurance of faith, because Christ has died to put away sin, the one thing that had previously prevented them doing this. If Christians could only pray when they were worthy to do so, they never would. The exhilarating fact is that the way is now open for every Christian to pray at any time, in any place and in any frame of mind. Whatever your situation, however you feel, whatever your problem, let nothing keep you back from prayer and from knowing that because of the death of Jesus on your behalf, you can have instant and constant access to your Father in heaven.

PRAISE THE LORD!

First and foremost, use this privilege to worship God and to praise his name. In the words of the psalmist, 'Great is the LORD and greatly to be praised, and his greatness is unsearchable' (Psalm 145:3). That being so, no Christian need ever run out of things to say when they pray!

The more you read your Bible, the more you will learn of the majesty, glory, holiness, greatness, wisdom, mercy and love of God; and the more you learn of these, the more you will find yourself agreeing with David when he says, 'Bless the LORD, O my soul, and all that is within me, bless his holy name!' (Psalm103:1).

But praise and worship should lead to thanksgiving. David says, 'Bless the LORD, O my soul, and forget not all his benefits' (Psalm 103:2). Paul says that we should be 'giving thanks always and for everything to God the Father in the name of our Lord Jesus Christ' (Ephesians 5:20). Just as the glory of God can never exhaust our praise, so the blessings of God can never exhaust our thanksgiving. Christians should have a gratitude attitude! Above all,

Christians should never tire of thanking God for his sending Jesus to be their Saviour, and should gladly join the apostle Paul in saying, 'Thanks be to God for his inexpressible gift!' (2 Corinthians 9:15).

CONFESSION IS GOOD FOR THE SOUL

No Christian can spend long praising God for his majesty and glory and thanking him for his goodness before sensing something of their own moral and spiritual shortcomings. The apostle John says bluntly, 'If we say we have no sin, we deceive ourselves, and the truth is not in us,' but he immediately adds this wonderful promise: 'If we confess our sins, [*God*] is faithful and just to forgive us our sins and to cleanse us from all unrighteousness' (1 John 1:8-9). We saw in Chapter 4 that in spite of being justified, our daily walk as Christians always falls short of God's holy standards, and we need to come to him daily in prayer to confess our sins and ask for his forgiveness. The word 'confess' means 'to name together' and to confess our sins means to agree with what God says about them. Confession is made to God, not to a priest, because God is the only one who can forgive our sins. Confession is always humbling, but if we openly acknowledge our sins of word, thought and deed, we can be assured of God's complete and free forgiveness.

THE PERFECT PRAYER

When his disciples asked Jesus how to pray, he replied with what we now call 'The Lord's Prayer', which broadly speaking asks for three things.

First, that God's glory might be recognized: 'Our Father in heaven, hallowed be your name, your kingdom come, your will be done, on earth as it is in heaven' (Matthew 6:9-10).

These three petitions are concerned with the honouring of God's name, the coming of his kingdom and the doing of his will. Later on in the same chapter Jesus says, 'Seek first the kingdom of God and his righteousness' (Matthew 6:33). Our priority in praying should be God-centred. Whenever you pray, make sure that your motives are right and that your overriding concern is God's glory, not your good.

Second, that God's goodness might be received: 'Give us this day our daily bread' (Matthew 6:11). This simple prayer acknowledges our total dependence on God, not least for the food we eat day by day. As Paul tells the people of Athens, '[*God*] himself gives to all mankind life and breath and everything' (Acts 17:25). Nothing is healthier for us than to accept that we are utterly dependent upon God, not only for our spiritual needs, but for every other need in life.

Third, that God's grace might be revealed. Forgive us our debts, as we also have forgiven our debtors. And lead us not into temptation, but deliver us from evil' (Matthew 6:12-13). Only by God's grace can we be forgiven, have a forgiving spirit towards others, be kept from yielding to temptation and delivered from the power of Satan (more about this in Chapter 13). Pulling all of this together tells us that above all else we should strive to be 'holy and blameless before [*God*]' (Ephesians 1:4).

Prayer is a God-given privilege, but we need to realize that God's timing is always perfect, and we must learn to trust him even when we cannot trace what he is doing (or feel that he is doing nothing). Delay is not the same as denial. Waiting for an answer is sometimes part of the answer, but Jesus teaches that we 'ought always to pray and not lose heart' (Luke 18:1). God only delays his answers when it is best to do so, and the delayed answer is for his glory and for our good. Make sure that you settle for that!

'MAYDAY!'

Taken from the French 'M'aider!' ('Help me!'), this is the international distress call, urgently asking for assistance—and there are sometimes situations when the same kind of prayer is needed. When Jesus was asleep on board his disciples' boat on the Sea of Galilee a sudden storm arose and threatened to drown them all. The terrified disciples woke him and cried, 'Save us, Lord; we are perishing' (Matthew 8:25.) Their need was serious and obvious, and their 'Mayday!' prayer was answered as Jesus immediately 'rebuked the winds and the sea, and there was a great calm' (Matthew 8:26).

Nothing ever takes God by surprise. With him, there are no unforeseen circumstances, no panic stations, and as he understands our frailty so well we can be assured that he is always tuned in on the 'Mayday!' frequency, ready and able to hear and answer our emergency calls. Nothing is out of ultimate control, because nothing is out of his control. No wonder the writer to the Hebrews says, 'Let us then with confidence draw near to the throne of grace, that we may receive mercy and find grace to help in time of need' (Hebrews 4:16).

The Christian is not only free to pray at any time and in any place, but also on any subject. Every detail of life can be taken to God in prayer, asking for his help, his blessing, his guidance, or his enabling. There is no issue so big that God cannot cope with it—'Is anything too hard for the LORD?' (Genesis 18:14)—and no issue so small that God does not care about it—'Even the hairs of your head are all numbered' (Matthew 10:30). This does not make praying easy. Even the apostle Paul admits, 'We do not know what to pray for as we ought'—yet he immediately adds, 'but the Spirit himself intercedes for us with groanings too deep for words. And he who searches hearts knows what is the mind of the Spirit, because the Spirit intercedes for the saints according to the will of God' (Romans 8:26-27). Only as the Holy Spirit helps us will we truly pray according to God's will. Ask him to do so, so that you will learn to pray in line with the 'good and acceptable and perfect' will of God (Romans 12:2). As you do, you will experience the truth of the Bible's promise that 'The prayer of a righteous person has great power as it is working' (James 5:16).

11

ONWARDS AND UPWARDS

THE BIBLE TEEMS WITH GUIDANCE, directions, examples, illustrations, warnings and promises aimed at helping Christians to make spiritual progress. There are times when God uses the Bible to help certain believers to make crucial decisions such as choosing a life partner or applying for a job. At other times he uses it to call them into full-time Christian ministry, or show them that they should offer to serve their local church in a particular way. These examples focus on individuals and at particular times, but there is one principle that applies to every Christian without exception and at all times. Whether young or old, a new Christian, or with many years as a member of God's family, '…this is the will of God, even your sanctification' (1 Thessalonians 4:3).

'Sanctification' is another of the Bible's great words, and we need to unwrap it before we go any further. Basically, 'to sanctify' has two meanings: firstly to separate or to set aside and secondly to make holy, or purify. In its first sense, it is used in the Old Testament about a great variety of things. For instance, in the story of creation we are told that God 'blessed the seventh day *and sanctified it*' (Genesis 2:3,

NKJV). This does not mean that it was a better day than any other, but that it was set apart in some special way.

The second use of the word comes mainly in the New Testament, where its meaning is again very clear. Paul writes, 'For God has not called us for impurity, but in holiness' (1 Thessalonians 4:7). As we will see shortly, there is also a 'set apart' element in this, but its emphasis is on practical, ongoing, day by day living in a way that is pleasing to God— the vocation of every Christian.

PERFECT—BUT PARTIAL

The Bible teaches that our sanctification is both perfect and partial. This sounds like a contradiction in terms, but it is not. A two-year-old child is a perfect human being, in the sense that it needs nothing else in order to make it a member of the human race. But it is far from being fully developed. If it is going to reach adulthood its cells, muscles, ligaments and limbs will have to grow. The same is true in the Christian life. Paul addresses one of his New Testament letters to 'the church of God that is in Corinth, to those *sanctified* in Christ Jesus, *called to be saints*' (1 Corinthians 1:2). In the first place, Paul says that these Christians are already sanctified. Later in the same letter he reminds some of his readers that although they have led thoroughly ungodly lives, '…you were washed, you were sanctified, you were justified in the name of the Lord Jesus Christ and by the Spirit of our God' (1 Corinthians 6:11). Theologians call this 'positional holiness', because this is the position in which every Christian stands in God's sight as far as his acceptance and salvation are concerned. In this sense, sanctification is not something towards which Christians aim, it is the position from which they begin; because they are 'in Christ', God accepts them as if they were perfect in every way.

Yet Paul adds that believers, already 'sanctified in Christ Jesus' are 'called to be saints' (in other words to become more and more sanctified as they grow in their Christian life). They cannot sit back and rest on the fact that God reckons them as perfect; they are called to do everything in their power to ensure that their daily lives are pleasing to God. For Christians today, holiness of life is something that must be constantly pursued by every means at their disposal: 'As obedient children, do not be conformed to the passions of your former ignorance, but as he who has called you is holy, you also be holy in all your conduct' (1 Peter 1:14-15).

A word of warning here; beware of being carried away by any teaching about sanctification that emphasizes morbid self-examination or emotionalism; Jesus was utterly holy, yet without a trace of any of these things. When Paul preached in a synagogue in Berea, we are told that his hearers not only 'received the word with all eagerness', but that they were also 'examining the Scriptures daily to see if these things were so' (Acts 17:11). If they did that with the teaching of an apostle, we should do the same today with the opinions of any other person, especially if they claim to have discovered the secret of how to become sanctified.

We saw in an earlier chapter that when a person becomes a Christian the Holy Spirit gives them a new nature. Yet the old nature remains; even the apostle Paul frankly admits, 'I know that nothing good dwells in me, that is, in my flesh' [*that is, his old, sinful nature*] (Romans 7:18). The result is that the Christian is a kind of walking civil war, with the two natures, the old and the new, fighting for the upper hand. Elsewhere, Paul explains this: 'For the desires of the flesh are against the Spirit, and the desires of the Spirit are against the flesh, for these are opposed to each other' (Galatians 5:17).

As we face this civil war, we need to grasp the fact that we can never win any of its battles (in other words, become more holy or sanctified) in our own strength, We are just as incapable of living a holy life as we were of giving ourselves spiritual birth in the first place, but with one important difference. Whereas the new birth is a sovereign work of God the Holy Spirit, in which we have no part at all, sanctification is something in which we are called to cooperate with him. Peter tells his readers that ['*God's*] divine power has granted to us all things that pertain to life and godliness', but then adds, 'For this very reason, *make every effort* to supplement your faith with virtue, and virtue with knowledge, and knowledge with self-control, and self-control with steadfastness, and steadfastness with godliness, and godliness with brotherly affection and brotherly affection with love' (2 Peter 1: 3,5-7). These statements pinpoint some of the things a holy life looks like, and they make it clear that this calls for us to work hard in using the strength God promises to give us.

In writing to the Christians at Philippi, the apostle Paul urges them to 'work out your own salvation' (Philippians 2:12). Because he is referring to salvation in the present tense we would not be twisting his meaning if we translated his words 'work at being holy', but he immediately adds, '…for it is God who works in you, both to will and to work for his good pleasure' (Philippians 2:13). Becoming more holy is not a DIY project. It is impossible for us to take a single step in the right direction without God's work in us. As the American preacher James Montgomery Boice put it, Paul means that 'a man is incapable of living out the kind of life that God requires of him, but that God is capable of living out that life in a man who yields to his Spirit.'

One of the things that should motivate us as we engage in holy warfare is the example Jesus set us. He sums up his entire life of obedience to his heavenly Father by saying 'I always do the things that are pleasing to him' (John 8:29).

The more we know of the majesty, holiness, power, glory and love of God, the more concerned we will be to please him in every part of our lives. When the Old Testament believer Joseph is tempted to commit adultery with his boss's wife, his immediate reply is, 'How can I do this great wickedness and sin against God?' (Genesis 39:9). The Christian should take exactly the same attitude in the face of every temptation to sin.

We find another powerful motive to aim for growing holiness when we reflect on what Jesus did to make it possible. The Bible says that 'we have been sanctified through the offering of the body of Jesus Christ once for all' (Hebrews 10:10). This obviously refers to that 'perfect' sanctification which we looked at earlier in this chapter, but the fact that Jesus went to such tremendous lengths to save us from the consequences of our sin should surely be a powerful incentive to live a holy life? His crucifixion shows us the appalling depth of our sin and the amazing depth of his love for us. How can we grasp that and be casual or careless about striving for the holiness of life he wants us to know?

Needless to say, the Bible is powerfully relevant here. In speaking to God, a psalmist asks, 'How can a young man keep his way pure?', then answers 'By guarding it according to your word' (Psalm 119:9). Praying for his disciples and for all succeeding generations of Christians, Jesus asks his heavenly Father to 'sanctify them in the truth; your word is truth' (John 17:17). The Christian who is making little or no spiritual progress is almost certainly one who is seriously neglecting the Bible. One who is gradually moving ahead is almost certainly one of whom it can be said that 'His delight is in the law of the LORD, and on his law he meditates day and night' (Psalm 1:2).

DOWN TO EARTH

Everything this chapter has said about living a holy life has been anchored to the Bible, and you might feel that it is all very theoretical, but this is not the case. The apostle Paul realizes that growing in holiness means life-long determination, discipline and perseverance: 'Forgetting what lies behind and straining forward to what lies ahead, I press on towards the goal for the prize of the upward call of God in Christ Jesus' (Philippians 3:13-14). The original Greek word translated 'straining forward' is one that would be used of an athlete striving as hard as possible to win a race— and as Christians we should be equally determined to do everything we can to get further down life's track than we have ever been before. Here are some of the ways you can do this:

Go much further than merely reading the Bible. One of the psalmists tells God, 'I have stored up your word in my heart that I might not sin against you' (Psalm 119:11). Think deeply about what you read, and try to memorize key statements, treasuring their truth so that you can call on them at times of temptation.

Carefully decide what you will allow yourself to see and your mind to feed on—especially before you turn on the TV or go online. This is massively important for the Christian and the influences involved have never been stronger or more pervasive. Dieters who find themselves looking at 'forbidden' foods are often unable to resist them. For Christians, the same principle applies. The mass media, including books, magazines, films, television and the internet pours out godless material that can have devastating effects on a person's thinking and behaviour. Be determined to guard your mind and follow the Bible's guidelines: 'Whatever is true, whatever is honourable, whatever is just, whatever is pure, whatever is lovely, whatever is commendable, if there is any excellence, if there is anything worthy of praise, think about these things' (Philippians 4:8).

Don't allow yourself excuses for sin. You will never break a habit if you constantly make exceptions to the rule. If you are serious about sanctification—and you should be—you will wage a personal daily war, with the Holy Spirit's help, against anything that is not pleasing to God.

Ask the Holy Spirit to show you *all* your bad habits. All of us have things we enjoy which we do not see as sin and would be reluctant to give up. Remember that in God's eyes there are no small sins. Ask God to sharpen your conscience so that you will more clearly see things that need to be changed and be ready to take action when he does.

Always bear in mind that the battle to be holy is a lifelong one. Temptations change as you grow older and what tempted you as a teenager may not tempt you later on in life, but something else will always take its place. The fight again sin will not be over until the day you die. The eighteenth-century preacher William Grimshaw realized this and said 'I expect to lay down my sword and my life together'—and you will find that the same is true for you.

EVENTUALLY...

Even if you are a relatively new Christian (and certainly if you have been one for years) you will be able to confirm that resisting temptation, avoiding sin and growing in holiness is not easy, nor is it a 'press button' experience. The old, fallen nature remains with us right until the end of our earthly journey. Never think that you can achieve in a single moment what God says will take a lifetime. We do not become holy in one moment by making Jesus Lord of our life; instead, we are called to be holy moment by moment because he already *is* Lord.

Writing to the Philippians about being conformed to Christ, Paul adds, *'Not that I have already obtained this or am already perfect,* but I press on to make it my own, because Christ Jesus has made me his own' (Philippians 3:12). Towards the end of his remarkable life, Paul acknowledged that he was by no means perfect, so you can safely ignore the extravagant claims of anyone who claims to have gone one better. *But we will be perfect one day!* The process of our sanctification will come to a glorious climax in the life to come. God's eternal purpose that we be 'conformed to the image of his Son' (Romans 8:29) will be realized, and when that happens the entire Christian church will stand in God's glorious presence, 'in splendour, without spot or wrinkle or any such thing, … holy and without blemish' (Ephesians 5:27).

As R.C.Sproul put it, ' There is no time lapse between our justification and the beginning of our sanctification… As soon as we truly believe, at that very instant, the process of becoming pure and holy is underway, and its future completion is certain.' More about that amazing future in our final chapter.

12

THE ENEMY

GOD HAS DELIVERED Christians from 'the domain of darkness' (Colossians 1:13), but it is important for us to realize that this domain still exists, ruled by the most extraordinary being in the whole universe other than God himself— the devil. To many people he is just a figment of the imagination, while to others he is a cartoon figure, a peppery old man with red cheeks and green eyes, and horns protruding out of his head—yet these are dangerous caricatures. In the Bible, a person's name often gives a clue to their nature or character, and this is certainly true of the devil. The title 'the devil' (Matthew 4:1), means an accuser or slanderer. He is often called 'Satan' (Job 1:6), meaning an adversary or opponent; elsewhere, he is specifically called 'your adversary' (1 Peter 5:8). Jesus calls him 'Beelzebul, the prince of demons' (Matthew 12:24), 'the ruler of this world' (John 14:30) and 'the evil one' (Matthew 13:19), and says he was 'a murderer' and 'a liar' (John 8:44). Paul identifies him as 'the god of this world' (2 Corinthians 4:4), 'Belial' (meaning 'worthlessness') (2 Corinthians 6:15) and 'the prince of the power of the air' (Ephesians 2:2). Nobody should read that horrendous list of names and still think of Satan in casual or light-hearted terms.

We are not told a great deal about his origin, but we have a clue when we hear Jesus saying, 'I saw Satan fall like lightning from heaven' (Luke 10:18). Another clue comes when Paul warns certain people about becoming 'puffed up with conceit' and running the risk of falling into 'the condemnation of the devil' (1 Timothy 3:6). These point to his having originally been a perfect angelic being created by God and living in heaven, but at some stage seeking to overthrow God and take over the rule of the universe, an insane rebellion that ended in his being cast out of God's presence. As the Bible also speaks of 'angels who did not stay within their own position of authority but left their proper dwelling' (Jude 6), it would seem that an unspecified number of other angels shared his sin and were swept out at the same time. We are not given any clear information about this, but when the Bible speaks of Satan's present activities, it often links them with 'the cosmic powers over this present darkness' and 'the spiritual forces of evil in the heavenly places' (Ephesians 6:12).

Although fallen from his original status, Satan is now the head of his own satanic kingdom, an untold number of evil spirits, (sometimes called 'demons' in the Bible) who carry out his diabolical activities. With this vast army at his disposal, he exercises unimaginable power in the world, and particularly over all those who are not Christians. Paul says that 'The god of this world has blinded the minds of the unbelievers, to keep them from seeing the light of the gospel of the glory of Christ, who is the image of God' (2 Corinthians 4:4). He even goes so far as to say that unbelievers are in 'the snare of the devil, after being captured by him to do his will' (2 Timothy 2:26). This confirms what Jesus told some of his enemies: 'You are of your father, the devil, and your will is to do your father's desires' (John 8:44). Satan is the ruler of a kingdom and the head of a vast family of people who (mostly without realizing it), carry out his wishes.

WARFARE

He is also the Christian's constant, merciless opponent. Peter warns believers, 'Your adversary the devil prowls around like a roaring lion, seeking someone to devour' (1 Peter 5:8). With the help of a host of unseen agents, he is engaged in total warfare against us, trying in every way possible to drag us into defeat, disobedience and sin. Here are some of his tactics:

First, *the surprise attack.* Walking on his palace roof late one afternoon, King David 'saw... a woman bathing, and the woman was very beautiful' (2 Samuel 11:2). In next to no time, he seduced her, got her pregnant, then concocted a scheme to have her husband murdered. Yet it all happened so quickly! Given time to think things through, we should expect believers to resist such obvious temptation, but a sudden, unexpected attack can prove fatally effective. Christians can never afford to drop their guard, to be careless, or to be over-confident. Speaking in the House of Commons in 1913 on the subject of naval defence, the then First Lord of the Admiralty Winston Churchill said, 'We must always be ready to meet at our average moment anything that any possible enemy might hurl against us at his selected moment.' Outside of the Bible, it would be difficult to imagine better advice than that.

Second, *the siege attack.* A stone that can hardly be scratched with a knife can be completely worn away by the slow, continuous dripping of water, and Christians who seem to cope very well with obvious and open temptation sometimes crack under constant pressure. This is almost certainly what happened In the case of Judas Iscariot, the disciples' honorary treasurer. Little by little, Satan laid siege to his heart. Firstly, there was the temptation to make a little money for himself on the side. Then came the first furtive finger in the till. Gradually, petty theft became a steady habit: John says bluntly, 'He was a thief, and having charge of the money bag he used to help himself to what was put into it' (John 12:6). Finally, he agreed to betray Jesus to the authorities for thirty pieces of silver and 'sought an opportunity to betray him' (Matthew 26:15-16). Check carefully that you are not letting Satan slowly and relentlessly erode your standards.

Third, *the subtle attack.* Satan is a master of disguise, and there are even times when he 'disguises himself as an angel of light' (2 Corinthians 11:14). If he can do that, he has no difficulty in making sin look innocent or amusing. The temptation of Adam and Eve is a perfect example of this. As a result of Satan's subtle insinuations, Eve saw the tree of the knowledge of good and evil not as something forbidden by God, but as 'good for food, and... a delight to the eyes, and... to be desired to make one wise' (Genesis 3:6). Yet instead of physical food, our first parents found spiritual poison; instead of satisfaction, they found shame; instead of unlimited pleasure, they found unspeakable pain. Beware of the subtle attack! Remember that if Satan can look like an angel, he can also make vice look like virtue and error like truth. Learn to test your thoughts, opinions, desires and assessment of suggestions and situations by the truth of God's Word, or you will run the risk of being caught out by Satan's subtlety.

THE BIG MATCH

The Bible records a dramatic face-to-face encounter between Jesus and Satan, and looking at this gives us further insight into the enemy's tactics.

The first temptation was this: 'If you are the Son of God, command these stones to become loaves of bread' (Matthew 4:3). Jesus had fasted for forty days and nights, so here was a clear temptation for him to use his power in order to satisfy his bodily appetite. But Jesus repelled Satan by telling him, 'Man shall not live by bread alone, but by every word that comes from the mouth of God' (Matthew 4:4). Satan knows all about our physical needs, urges and appetites, and exactly when and how to strike.

The second was this: Taking Jesus to the highest point of the temple in Jerusalem, he said, 'If you are the Son of God, throw yourself down,' craftily adding part of a quotation from Psalm 91, in which God promised, 'He will command his angels concerning you, and on their hands they will bear you up, lest you strike your foot against a stone' (Matthew 4:5-6). Yet he deliberately left out the very important qualifying words 'to guard you in all your ways.' God's promise was not that he would protect a person regardless of what they did, but only when they were obeying his will. Jesus immediately responded with an accurate and relevant quotation from Deuteronomy 6:16: 'You shall not put the LORD your God to the test' (Matthew 4:7). Beware of twisting the Bible's teaching to suit your own ends. You can lay hold of God's promises if you walk in his ways, and the Bible shows you what they are.

The third was this: Showing Jesus all the kingdoms of the world, Satan promised, 'All these I will give you, if you will fall down and worship me' (Matthew 4:9). Jesus could avoid the agony of his crucifixion if only he would abandon his mission and worship Satan instead. But to do that would be to disobey the clear command of his Father, and Jesus replied in a flash, 'Be gone, Satan! For it is written: "You shall worship the Lord your God, and him only shall you serve"' (Matthew 4:10).

This last temptation was a blatant and brutal assault, and we can be sure that Satan will not spare us from the same kind of attack. Christians should learn from all three temptations and the way Jesus repelled them, and notice especially that in every case Jesus did so by using truth from God's Word.

THE LAST WORD

The Bible not only outlines Satan's past and tells us of his present activities and tactics; it also charts his future, and tells us that he is on a collision course with ultimate judgement and condemnation. Although he is still able to exercise tremendous power, the Bible says 'he knows that his time is short!' (Revelation 12:12). His influence is limited not only by God's providence, but also by his timetable, which promises to Christians that the day will come when God will finally 'crush Satan under your feet' (Romans 16:20). Elsewhere, we are told that 'eternal fire' is 'prepared for the devil and his angels' (Matthew 25:41). In an indescribable moment of final judgement Satan and all his host will be 'thrown into the lake of fire and sulphur... and they will be tormented day and night forever and ever' (Revelation 20:10). Satan's reign of terror will finally be over, while all those who have trusted Jesus Christ as their Saviour will rejoice for ever in 'new heavens and a new earth in which righteousness dwells' (2 Peter 3:13).

13

THE BATTLE

IN THE FILM *FORREST GUMP*, the lead character (played by Tom Hanks) remembers his mother telling him that life 'was like a box of chocolates. You never know what you're gonna get.' It is difficult to argue with that, especially as the Bible tells us that 'you do not know what tomorrow will bring' (James 4:14). Yet as we go through life, some things are certain—and one of these is temptation. As Paul puts it, 'No temptation has overtaken you that is not common to man' (1 Corinthians 10:13).

Having seen something of Satan's origin, career, tactics and destiny, it will be helpful to take a closer look at the question of temptation, and we should begin by understanding that while every temptation is a test, not every test is a temptation. In a nutshell, God tests us in order to help us to stand, whereas Satan tempts us in order to make us fall. All our circumstances are under God's sovereign control, and nothing can touch us without God's permission. He is never the direct cause of any temptation or any incitement to commit sin: 'Let no one say when he is tempted, "I am being tempted by God," for God cannot be tempted with evil, and he himself tempts no one' (James 1:13).

Many Christians begin to lose the battle against temptation by thinking that nobody else shares their experience, but this is not the case, and this danger can be avoided by grasping three straightforward facts.

First, temptation is not removed when a person becomes a Christian. In fact, temptations can become more intense, for the obvious reason that as soon as a person becomes a friend of God he becomes the sworn enemy of Satan. Second, temptation is not repelled from the Christian by a life of isolation, an act of dedication, or a vow of consecration. There is no spiritual crisis or 'blessing' or 'experience' that can deliver the Christian from further attacks. Third, temptation is not reduced by a Christian's spiritual progress. No growth in maturity will guarantee that Satan will stand off or reduce the frequency or ferocity of his attacks.

It is important to grasp all of this, because it is easy to feel that constant temptation (especially in the same area) must mean you are a failure as a Christian and you must have grieved God in such a way that he has deserted you. From there, it is easy to think that you might as well give up, back down, or sell out. These are all devil-sent lies. It is also important to understand that temptation is not sin, nor is it an indication of failure. No man on earth was subject to more constant attacks from Satan than Jesus. He was 'in every respect... tempted as we are, *yet without sin*' (Hebrews 4:15). That single statement should immediately put all of your temptation in its right perspective.

WAR ON ALL FRONTS

No section of the army is more important than the Intelligence Corps which finds the identity, capability and intention of the enemy and keeps its own forces informed of the situation on all fronts. In the Christian life, it is similarly important that we should know the areas in which Satan operates, and we can note some of them here.

The moral front. All sin is immoral, but we usually think of morality in terms of the physical, and especially the sexual. Sex is one of God's most precious gifts, not only as a means of reproducing human life, but as a total expression of love and for the giving and receiving of mutual strength and comfort between a man and his wife. Yet Satan has twisted and warped this lovely gift beyond recognition and used it to torment and wreck the lives of millions of people, and we now live at a time when moral absolutes have been replaced by personal opinion and popular culture. Outrages against even common decency in books and magazines, radio, television, the internet, computer games and social media provide sickening evidence of this.

This moral mayhem rides roughshod over fundamental biblical standards. One is that 'A man shall leave his father and his mother and hold fast to his wife, and they shall become one flesh' (Genesis 2:24). That means *purity before marriage.* Another says, 'You shall not commit adultery' (Exodus 20:14). That means *purity within marriage.* Again, the Bible says to the Christian, 'Flee from sexual immorality. Every other sin a person commits is outside the body, but the sexually immoral person sins against his own body. Or do you not know that your body is a temple of the Holy Spirit within you, whom you have from God? You are not your own, for you were bought with a price. So glorify God in your body' (1Corinthians 6:18-20). That means *purity outside of marriage.* Whether you are young or old, single, in a relationship or married, be constantly on the alert for temptation along the moral front, and remember that it can be directed to the mind, the will, the desire or the imagination, as well as to the body.

The last three paragraphs have additional relevance in today's cultural climate, in which homosexuality, lesbianism, same-sex marriage, gender fluidity (with people claiming to have no gender or to have a fluctuating gender or to be other-gendered) are increasingly believed to be morally acceptable. Yet all of these are in direct conflict with the Bible's teaching that gender identity is determined by God-given biological design, not by self-perception or romantic choice. The Bible speaks with serious clarity about those who have 'given themselves up to sensuality, greedy to practise every kind of impurity' and urges God's people to be 'renewed in the spirit of your minds, and to put on the new self, created after the likeness of God in true righteousness and holiness' (Ephesians 4:19, 23-24).

The material front. Man is basically greedy; he has a passion to possess—and Satan knows it. Materialism is a deadly danger, especially in the present age of aggressive advertising. There is a fine line between a sensible concern for a reasonable living standard and an unhealthy appetite for an increasing accumulation of 'things.' Every Christian should keep a sharp lookout for danger signals in this whole area. 'Keeping up with the Joneses' might result in getting away from God!

The Bible nowhere condemns riches and material possessions as such, but it gives clear warnings that, like sex, they are dangerous and disastrous if handled wrongly. Paul warns, 'But those who desire to be rich fall into temptation, into a snare, into many senseless and harmful desires that plunge people into ruin and destruction. For the love of money is a root of all kinds of evils. It is through this craving that some have wandered away from the faith and pierced themselves with many pangs' (1 Timothy 6:9-10). You have been warned! Get the whole question of money and material possessions in the right perspective. Remember that you are responsible to God for all the gifts he allows you to have, and bear in mind that 'The things that are seen are transient, but the things that are unseen are eternal' (2 Corinthians 4:18).

The mental front. This is another area in which Satan makes huge inroads into some people's lives. Worry, doubt, tension, fear, stress, pressure and anxiety are found all over society, and every Christian should be on his guard against them. Christians who miss out on fellowship with other believers, who are satisfied with a casual relationship with Jesus, who let their prayer life shrivel away, or who are too lazy to apply themselves to studying the Bible, will find their mental molehills slowly turning into mountains. Beware of this, and of your usefulness as a Christian dwindling disastrously. Get into the healthy habit of 'casting all your anxieties on [*God*], because he cares for you' (1 Peter 5:7).

The personal front. There is one factor which has a part to play in virtually every sin, even when it is not recognized as such, and that is pride. If pride can take Satan from heaven to hell, it can certainly take you from your present position into a place of failure, disobedience, defeat and shame. Satan is fully aware of this, and if you want to grow as a Christian, if you want to avoid barrenness, emptiness and uselessness, begin by taking time to study the Bible's teaching on the subject of pride and humility. Look especially at the life of Jesus, and pray constantly for grace to 'walk humbly with your God' (Micah 6:8). Above all, learn to live on the basis of this great promise: 'Humble yourselves before the Lord, and he will exalt you' (James 4:10).

THE WAY TO WIN

We have already noted Paul's words that 'No temptation has overtaken you that is not common to man,' but he goes on to say, 'God is faithful; and he will not let you be tempted beyond your ability, but with the temptation he will also provide the way of escape, that you may be able to endure it' (1 Corinthians 10:13). This tells us that there is no escape from temptation, but also that there is no excuse for sin. By his sovereign overruling of all Satan's activities, God has promised that with every temptation will come a way out, by which his people can triumph over it. There is certainly no slick 'ABC of holy living' that we can tick off like a shopping list, but the Bible points us to several vital pieces of equipment we can use in fighting the enemy.

The first is *vigilance*. Paul says, 'So then let us not sleep, as others do, but let us keep awake and be sober' (1 Thessalonians 5:6). We saw in Chapter 12 that Satan 'prowls around like a roaring lion, seeking someone to devour' (1 Peter 5:8), which means that we dare not live a slipshod, careless life, but always be on our guard, especially in areas where we know we are particularly vulnerable. The permanent presence of the old nature guarantees that in the Christian life there is no victory without vigilance.

The second is *prayer*. Jesus tells us, 'Watch and pray that you may not enter into temptation. The spirit indeed is willing, but the flesh is weak' (Matthew 26:41). Prayer is the vital link between man's need and God's power. As the prophet Isaiah puts it, '[*God*] gives power to the faint, and to him who has no might he increases strength. Even youths shall faint and be weary, and young men shall fall exhausted; but they who wait for the LORD shall renew their strength; they shall mount up with wings like eagles; they shall run and not be weary; they shall walk and not faint' (Isaiah

40:29-31). To face temptation without prayer is like going into a nuclear war armed with a peashooter. Look again at Chapter 10, learn the discipline of daily prayer and prove the effectiveness of emergency prayer!

The third is *faith*. John writes, 'This is the victory that has overcome the world—our faith' (1 John 5:4), while the writer of Hebrews says that in running the race of life we are to be 'looking to Jesus, the founder and perfecter of our faith' (Hebrews 12:2). Even prayer will not be effective if it lacks faith and is just an empty form of words. As the English preacher Thomas Watson put it, 'God hears no more than the heart speaks; if the heart is dumb, God will certainly be deaf.' We must pray earnestly and with faith. The quality of our faith affects the quality of our life and is a crucial factor in the outcome of the temptations and testing we face day by day. It was in the very context of temptation and sin that the disciples cried out to Jesus, 'Increase our faith!' (Luke 17:5). You should do the same.

The fourth is the equipment the Bible calls '*the whole armour of God*'. Paul writes: 'Finally, be strong in the Lord and in the strength of his might. Put on the whole armour of God, that you may be able to stand against the schemes of the devil. For we do not wrestle against flesh and blood, but against the rulers, against the authorities, against the cosmic powers over this present darkness, against the spiritual forces of evil in the heavenly places. Therefore take up the whole armour of God, that you may be able to withstand in the evil day, and having done all, to stand firm. Stand therefore, having fastened on *the belt of truth*, and having put on *the breastplate of righteousness,* and, as shoes for your feet, having put on the readiness given by *the gospel of peace*. In all circumstances take up *the shield of faith,* with which you can extinguish all the flaming darts of the evil one; and take *the helmet of salvation*, and *the sword of the Spirit*, which is *the word of God,* praying at all times in the Spirit, with *all prayer and supplication*' (Ephesians 6:10-18). Go carefully over these pieces of equipment, find out what they mean, and make sure you use all the armour God has provided for you to resist temptation.

The fifth is *determined resistance.* James urges us, 'Submit yourselves therefore to God. Resist the devil, and he will flee from you' (James 4:7). Here is a clear promise that temptation can be overcome, but only when Christians are prepared to yield to God and to resist Satan at every point. Whole-hearted obedience and whole-hearted resistance are the twin secrets of success. Paul was able to say, 'I can do all things through him who strengthens me' (Philippians 4:13). Over 2,000 later, you have the God-given privilege of being able to say the same thing.

14

THE GREATER POWER

In a fascinating Old Testament incident, the pagan King of Syria set out to capture the prophet Elisha. A whistleblower told him Elisha was in the city of Dothan, so one night the king surrounded the city with soldiers. When Elisha's servant got up early the next morning and saw them, he rushed back to Elisha and asked, 'What shall we do?' The prophet replied, 'Do not be afraid, for those who are with us are more than those who are with them' (2 Kings 6:16). He then prayed that his servant would realize that God's resources easily outnumbered those of the King of Syria, and that he would protect and rescue them—and in a remarkable way (no space for details here) he did.

Elisha's response to his servant came to my mind as I began to write this chapter. The last two have been about Satan, his vast army, his powerful resources and his subtle tactics, and Christians could be intimidated if they spent too much time thinking about this—but (to adapt Elisha's words) 'He who is with us is greater than those who are with him.' This greater person is God the Holy Spirit, eternally and sovereignly co-equal with God the Father and God the Son.

This makes two fundamental facts clear. The first is that the Holy Spirit is not merely a quality, an influence or a power, but a living person. In the Bible, we read of him speaking to people, working with others and sending some into particular spheres of Christian service, and we can settle the issue by reading just one sentence spoken by Jesus. Shortly before his death, he promises his disciples that after his own resurrection and ascension the Holy Spirit will come to them, then adds, 'When the Spirit of truth comes, he will guide you into all the truth, for he will not speak on his own authority, but whatever he hears he will speak, and he will declare to you the things that are to come' (John 16:13). The fact that the words 'he' and 'his' occur six times in one sentence proves the Spirit's personality once and for all.

The second fact is that the Holy Spirit is not merely a person, but a divine person. The Bible teaches that he is *God*, not merely a supernatural being who acts on God's behalf. For example, *statements made by God in the Old Testament are said in the New Testament to have been made by the Holy Spirit*. The apostle Paul introduces a quotation from the prophet Isaiah 6:9-10 with the words, 'The Holy Spirit was right in saying to your fathers through Isaiah the prophet...' (Acts 28:25). Then *qualities which clearly belong only to God are attributed to the Holy Spirit.* He is present everywhere: David asks, 'Where shall I go from your Spirit? Or where shall I flee from your presence?' (Psalm 139:7). He has divine power. When Jesus' mother Mary asked how, as a virgin, she could give birth to the promised Messiah the angel told her, 'The Holy Spirit will come upon you, and the power of the Most High will overshadow you' (Luke 1:35). *He is possessed of total knowledge*: 'The Spirit searches everything, even the depths of God' (1Corinthians 2:10). We are told that *sinning against the Holy Spirit is sinning against God.* Some early Christians agreed to sell up their property and pool the proceeds, but when Ananias and his wife Sapphira kept back some money for themselves, Peter asked him, 'Ananias, why has Satan filled your heart to lie to the Holy Spirit and to keep back for yourself part of the proceeds of the land? . . . You have not lied to man but to God' (Acts 5:3-4).

NOTHING WITHOUT THE SPIRIT

Without the Holy Spirit's work, we would have no sense of God, no means of coming to know him and no power to obey him. Only the Holy Spirit can 'convict the world concerning sin and righteousness and judgement' (John 16:8). Without the work of the Holy Spirit, we will never be conscious of our spiritual condition and need. It is only by the Holy Spirit that we can be born again and brought to repentance and saving faith; our first steps in the Christian life were 'begun by the Spirit' (Galatians 3:3). It is the Holy Spirit who introduces a person into God's family: 'For in one Spirit we were all baptized into one body' [*that is, the true Christian church*] (1 Corinthians 12:13). A Christian may not always be conscious of the Holy Spirit's presence, but he would not even be a Christian in his absence.

Our assurance of salvation is the work of the Holy Spirit: 'The Spirit himself bears witness with our spirit that we are children of God' (Romans 8:16). We grow in godliness as we are 'being transformed into [*the Lord's*] image from one degree of glory to another' and this 'comes from the Lord who is the Spirit' (2 Corinthians 3:18). Virtues such as love, joy, peace, patience, kindness, goodness, faithfulness, gentleness, self-control are called 'the fruit of the Spirit'

(Galatians 5:22). The way to resist temptation successfully is to be strengthened 'with power through [*God's*] Spirit' (Ephesians 3:16). Finally, God tells us that the only way to serve him effectively is 'by my Spirit' (Zechariah 4:6).

THE GIFTS

Many Christians are led to believe that they should be seeking for some dramatic encounter with the Holy Spirit which will result in their receiving one or more exciting spiritual gifts, such as the ability to prophesy or to speak with 'tongues' and that this will be evidence of God's special blessing on their lives. Two key New Testament passages will point us in the right direction here. The apostle Paul tells the Corinthian Christians, 'Now there are varieties of gifts, but the same Spirit; and there are varieties of service, but the same Lord; and there are varieties of activities, but it is the same God who empowers them all in everyone' (1 Corinthians 12:4-6). In the second passage, he tells Christians in Rome, 'Having gifts that differ according to the grace given to us, let us use them: if prophecy, in proportion to our faith; if service, in our serving; the one who teaches, in his teaching; the one who exhorts, in his exhortation; the one who contributes, in generosity; the one who leads, with zeal; the one who does acts of mercy, with cheerfulness' (Romans 12:6- 8). From these two passages, we can establish these facts:

Firstly, *not all the gifts of the Spirit are exotic or sensational.* The prospect of things like prophecy or speaking in tongues might well sound exciting, but the gift of tongues was a supernatural gift given to the apostles for the purpose of evangelism in the early church, while prophecy was used by God to reveal his mind and purposes to his people before they had his written Word. Today, we have the complete

Bible as God's full and sufficient revelation. What is more, as the British author Brian Edwards reminds us, speaking in a language with no intelligible meaning, is 'more of a religious phenomenon than a Christian one. It is found in many world religions and cults and even first century paganism experienced it.' This is not the amazing gift that enabled the apostles to preach the gospel in such a way that all their hearers heard it in their own language. As Brian Edwards adds, 'God allowed certain gifts to fill the gap so that he could speak directly to his people. When all the New Testament was written down, the gifts that gave direct revelation from God were withdrawn or at least greatly limited.'

Secondly, *not every Christian is expected to have every one of the gifts mentioned.* In both passages Paul speaks very clearly of differing gifts being given to different people. A Christian who possesses one particular gift, or who has it in an unusual measure, is wrong to insist that their condition is the norm for which others should strive.

Thirdly, *the gifts of the Spirit are not ours for the asking.* While all of the gifts are 'empowered by one and the same Spirit,' he 'apportions to each one individually as he wills' (1 Corinthians 12:11). The Holy Spirit deals with us as individuals according to his wisdom and not according to our wishes. These gifts are not rewards, and a Christian's true spiritual quality is to be judged by his graces, not by his gifts.

Fourthly, *the gifts of the Spirit are never for our own personal enjoyment.* In the Old Testament, only one person is specifically said to have been 'filled… with the Spirit of God' (Exodus 31:3). This was Bezalel, and the only recorded expression of this was the practical help he gave to building a tabernacle in the desert. It is also important to notice that serving, teaching, giving and works of mercy are also included in the list of gifts. When the early church chose seven men 'full of the Spirit and of wisdom' (Acts 6:3), it was not in order to perform some sensational ministry, but to oversee the distribution of supplementary funds to certain widows. The gifts of the Spirit are never meant for the Christian's own satisfaction, but always for the good of the church: 'As each has received a gift, use it to serve one another, as good stewards of God's varied grace' (1 Peter 4:10). Make sure that your gifts are being used in this way.

BEING FILLED

In the New Testament we are told, 'Do not grieve the Holy Spirit of God' (Ephesians 4:30), and in context the inference is that the Holy Spirit is grieved by any kind of unholy conduct. We are also told, 'Do not quench the Spirit' (1 Thessalonians 5:19). The Holy Spirit is like a purifying flame in the life of the church and we are solemnly warned against trying to dampen this down. We are also commanded to 'walk by the Spirit' (Galatians 5:16), or, as we might put it, 'keep in step with the Spirit.' This speaks of the need for obedience to everything the Holy Spirit reveals to us.

All these commands flow out of this crucially important one: 'Do not get drunk with wine, for that is debauchery, but *be filled with the Spirit*' (Ephesians 5:18), and we can get to its meaning by noticing three things about the phrase 'be filled.'

Firstly, it is *plural*. Just as drunkenness is forbidden for all Christians, so the command to be filled with the Spirit is for us all. The fullness of the Spirit is not something reserved for full-time ministers, or mature believers. It is available for us all, just as a tree's life-giving sap is available to fill the tiniest twig as well as the biggest branch. Secondly, it is *passive*. It is not something we do, but means 'Let the Spirit fill you.' This implies yielding ourselves unreservedly to him. Thirdly, it is always *present*, not a once-and-for-all experience; God wants us to know a continuous filling.

Just as our lungs are kept full of fresh air as we continue breathing, so we are constantly to expose every part of our daily life to the Holy Spirit's transforming ministry.

15

FINDING THE WAY

LIFE IS NOT A LOTTERY, so knowing and doing God's will is hugely important, yet an Old Testament writer asks the obvious question 'A man's steps are from the LORD; *how then can man understand his way?*' (Proverbs 20:24). This chapter answers that question.

Some Christians expect some kind of special revelation. Perhaps as the result of reading a startling incident in the Bible, or hearing someone's remarkable story, they expect God to speak to them through dreams or visions, unusual circumstances or in some other spectacular way. While we dare not try to limit the ways in which God may reveal his will to a Christian, his normal methods of guidance are far from spectacular.

For instance, one of God's gifts to Christians is a growing ability to discern whether a thing is right or wrong. Their conscience becomes increasingly sensitive and their judgement increasingly reliable. Every Christian should praise God for a growing ability to know the essential but sometimes subtle difference between right and wrong, as it is one of the greatest means of guidance that we can possibly have. If a thing is right, do it; if it is doubtful, question it; if it is wrong, avoid it.

God also expects us to use our common sense. We are not to switch off our minds and wait for some direct and unusual guidance before we act. We fulfil our daily responsibilities at home, at work, at school, college, university or elsewhere without any special revelation from God. The businessman whose office opens at 9 a.m. does not spend time gazing into space from 7.30 onwards waiting for God to guide his next move. The parent with a sick child, a hungry family or a mounting pile of household chores has no need to search the Bible for direct instructions.

PRINCIPLES

When some of his listeners express astonishment at what he is saying, Jesus tells them, 'My teaching is not mine, but his who sent me. *If anyone's will is to do God's will, he will know whether the teaching is from God* or whether I am speaking on my own authority' (John 7:16-17). The words I have emphasized are crucial. God does not waste truth on those unwilling to receive it, or give guidance to those determined not to follow it. Our fundamental responsibility in the matter of guidance is to be willing to obey God's will, whatever it may be, wherever it may lead and whatever it may cost.

Almost every time I am asked a question about guidance I turn the enquirer to these pivotal words: '[*God*] leads the humble in what is right and teaches the humble his way' (Psalm 25:9). The people God promises to guide are defined as 'the humble' and one of the clearest explanations of 'humble' comes in another of the psalms, where God says, 'I will instruct you and teach you in the way you should go; I will counsel you with my eye upon you. Be not like a horse or a mule, without understanding, which must be curbed with bit and bridle, or it will not stay near you' (Psalm 32:8-9). Until it is broken in, a horse is naturally headstrong and independent, while a mule tends to be stubborn and obstinate. The horse has to be restrained from running wild; the mule has to be pushed and prodded before it will move at all—and we are not to be like either of them. In order to claim the promise of God's guidance, you must neither dash ahead of him in self-centred enthusiasm, nor lag behind in hesitant unbelief. Instead, you must be willing not only to go in God's direction, but to do so at God's speed and in God's time.

Another bedrock principle on the question of guidance comes in this Old Testament statement: 'Trust in the LORD with all your heart, and do not lean on your own understanding. In all your ways acknowledge him, and he will make straight your paths' (Proverbs 3:5-6). Here is another clear promise of guidance, but again it is conditional. God promises to give further guidance to those who are already obeying him. Before setting out on a 100-mile car journey by night along unlit country roads you would switch on the headlights, which would illuminate, say, fifty yards of the road in front of you. All of the rest of the journey would be in total darkness, and only as you began to move along the road would the area beyond that initial fifty yards come into vision. Only as we are obedient to that part of God's will which he has revealed to us will we be given any further revelation. God only promises to give more light to those who walk in the light they have. If you are frustrated at not knowing God's will in some area of your life, could it be because you are being disobedient over some issue that he has already made clear?

GUIDELINES

We can now turn to look at some of the usual ways in which God guides the Christian, and the first is unquestionably his own Word, the Bible. Using the same picture of illumination, the psalmist says, 'Your word is a lamp to my feet and a light to my path' (Psalm 119:105). The Bible is God's infallible and unchanging Word and as such it can be trusted at all times and in all situations. It does not give detailed guidance on every situation that crops up in your life, but it does contain all the essential principles to guide and govern your living. It is not like an ordnance survey map, showing every minute geographical detail, but it is a perfectly accurate map of the whole area to be covered, with the main roads clearly marked. Within the pages of the Bible you will discover all that you need to know about God, man, sin, salvation, holiness, death and the life beyond.

Then how should we use the Bible in the matter of guidance? Certainly not as a 'lucky dip,' opening the Bible at random and hoping that a verse will stand out of the page and answer all our problems. I have a friend who says that his Bible naturally falls open at Judges 3 in the Old Testament and 2 Thessalonians 2 in the New Testament, but he knows that this is not guidance but a faulty binding! There are certainly times when 'out of the blue' God impresses a text so vividly on a Christian's heart that they are sure they are being divinely guided, but this is not God's usual method. We should seek to conduct our lives along the principles of 'the whole counsel of God' (Acts 20:27) and not by bits and pieces picked out at moments of sudden need. Nor should we wait for a crisis to come before looking to the Bible for guidance. Before radar was available, the captains of ships using the notorious Inner Passage off the coast of British Columbia and Alaska negotiated the hundreds of miles of tortuous seaway with scarcely an accident. They steered their ships through the changing tides and fogs by using their ships' sirens. They judged the distance from the nearest cliff face by noting the time it took the siren's echo to reach them. Even in dense fog they were able to do this because they had already done it many times in clear weather. The Christian best able to steer his way safely through dark and difficult times is the one who has made a constant habit of studying the Bible and storing its truth in his mind and heart.

The Bible gives us the next positive way in which we can know the guidance of God: 'If any of you lacks wisdom, let him ask God, who gives generously to all without reproach, and it will be given him' (James 1:5). The Amplified Bible translates part of that sentence, 'let him ask of the giving God.' God not only has a plan for our lives, but he is willing to reveal it to us. Prayer is not like squeezing information out of a reluctant stranger, but rather it is a confident request made to a wise, loving and generous Father.

Jesus points us to another important factor in knowing God's will. When he promises his disciples that after his own death the Holy Spirit will come to them, he adds, 'When the Spirit of truth comes, he will guide you into all the truth' (John 16:13). In the immediate context, this promise had to do with doctrine, but as we see later in the New Testament it goes beyond that. At one point, the apostle Paul and his companions are 'forbidden by the Holy Spirit to speak the word in Asia' (Acts 16:6). Then we are told, 'When they had come up to Mysia, they attempted to go into Bithynia, but the Spirit of Jesus did not allow them' (Acts 16:7). We could loosely paraphrase this (and lose nothing of its meaning) by saying, 'They tried again and again to go into Bithynia, but the Holy Spirit put his foot down and said, "No!"' We are not told why this happened, but Paul and his friends were obviously convinced that the Holy Spirit was speaking to them. Later, following (in this case) a remarkable vision, Paul's companion Luke says that they immediately 'sought to go on into Macedonia, concluding that God had called us to preach the gospel to them' (Acts 16:10-11). They came to a place free from obstacles only after the Holy Spirit had put other obstacles in their way.

The Bible says that Christians should habitually be 'led by the Spirit of God' (Romans 8:14), but we need to beware of treating all 'feelings' as if they are the voice of the Holy Spirit. In another context, but equally true here, John says, 'Do not believe every spirit, but test the spirits to see whether they are from God' (1 John 4:1). One sure way of doing this is to remember that the Holy Spirit never guides contrary to the Bible's teaching. To give one simple example, the Holy Spirit will never guide a Christian to marry a non-Christian, because the Bible says, 'Do not be unequally yoked with unbelievers' (2 Corinthians 6:14). Christians who say they 'feel led' to do such a thing are rejecting the authority of God's Word.

One final thing about guidance. As we have seen in the case of Paul and his friends in Asia, guidance is not always instant. For his own wise purposes, God sometimes delays revealing his will, even on an important issue, but because 'his way is perfect' (Psalm 18:30), you should always be grateful when he does. Just as a glass of cloudy water would become clear when you waited for the sediment to settle, so many of your uncertain situations will only become clarified as you allow God time to work and to speak. There may be times in your life when urgent, immediate action is needed, and God will never fail you in the hour of crisis. But there will be more situations than you think when you will need to follow David's God-given advice: 'Wait for the LORD; be strong, and let your heart take courage; wait for the LORD!' (Psalm 27:14).

16

TELL THE WORLD!

EARLY IN THE GOSPEL NARRATIVE, we read that Jesus 'went up on the mountain and called to him those whom he desired… (whom he also named apostles) so that they might be with him and he might send them out to preach' (Mark 3:13-14). Those early disciples were first called by Jesus to be with him and then sent out to share with the world the good news of salvation. They were called in and sent out—and so is every Christian in the world today.

THE EYEWITNESSES

For many years I worked in and around the Law Courts on the Channel Island of Guernsey, and came to know the importance of reliable witnesses in establishing a case. Someone who began his statement by saying he heard that a friend of a neighbour was told something or other would soon be dismissed by the judge! A witness need not be highly intelligent, widely read, impressive in appearance, or eloquent in speech, but it is essential that they give an accurate personal account. This principle comes across clearly in the New Testament. With an obvious reference to what happened when he, James and John saw Jesus transfigured on the mountain-top (as recorded in Mark 9), Peter writes, 'We did not follow cleverly devised myths when we made known to you the power and coming of our Lord Jesus Christ, but we were eyewitnesses of his majesty' (2 Peter 1:16), while in an earlier letter he calls himself 'a witness of the sufferings of Christ' (1 Peter 5:1). John begins the first of his letters in the same impressive way: 'That which was from the beginning, which we have heard, which we have seen with our eyes, which we looked upon and have touched with our hands, concerning the word of life... that which we have seen and heard we proclaim also to you' (1 John 1:1-3). And the meaning of what they saw in the flesh, you and every other Christian have since seen by faith. You have seen yourself as a guilty sinner. You have seen God's amazing love in providing a way of salvation. You have seen his justice satisfied in the death of his Son and you have seen that your sins have been cancelled by his sacrifice. You have witnessed these things with the eye of faith—and you are called to bear witness.

GOD'S GOSSIPS

Christians who think that witnessing to the truth of the gospel is best done by those in full-time ministry could not be further from the truth, and there is a great New Testament example to show this. In the early days of the church 'there arose... a great persecution against the church in Jerusalem, and they were all scattered throughout the regions of Judea and Samaria, *except the apostles* ... Now those who were scattered went about preaching the word' (Acts 8:1,4). The important thing to notice here is that the apostles, (the 'professionals'), remained in Jerusalem. It was the rank and file members of the church who were scattered abroad who preached the gospel wherever they went. Historians say that one of the greatest reasons for the success of the early church was the way in which ordinary Christians shared the good news of their faith with other people. There is no substitute for the public preaching of the gospel, and today's digital age has brought about a revolution in the manner and speed at which millions can now be reached all over the world. However, there is no escaping the personal responsibility of individual Christians to share the gospel with others and it is at this level that some of the most effective, penetrating and lasting evangelistic impact is made. Sharing the gospel with others is not always easy, but never be ashamed or afraid to 'gossip the gospel.' You will be surprised how often God gives you the right word for the right person at the right time.

Some Christians who are reluctant to speak to others about their faith make the excuse, 'I am a practical person, and I feel that the most important thing is to let my life speak'—but this misses an important point. Of course it is important that the quality of our lives should be such that people will be made to think; Jesus says, 'Let your light shine before others, so that they may see your good works and give glory to your Father who is in heaven' (Matthew 5:16). Yet a Christian is not only to be a person of good works, but of good words. Let me illustrate. Your best friend is suffering from a severe, painful rash. He tells you about the treatment he has tried without success. You have had the same rash and found the cure for it. You can carry on being a good friend by supporting and encouraging him in his discomfort, but unless you tell him of the cure he remains in pain. Your 'good works' need to be followed by 'good words.'

The same is true in communicating the gospel. Paul tells the Ephesians, 'In him you also, *when you heard the word of truth,* the gospel of your salvation, and believed in him, were sealed with the promised Holy Spirit' (Ephesians 1:13).

Writing to the Romans, he repeats the Old Testament prophet Joel's promise, 'Everyone who calls on the name of the Lord will be saved,' but immediately adds, 'But how are they to call on him in whom they have not believed? And how are they to believe in him of whom they have never heard? And how are they to hear without someone preaching? And how are they to preach unless they are sent?' (Romans 10:13-15). And to clinch the point, he then says, 'Faith comes from hearing, and hearing through the word of Christ' (Romans 10:17). In genuine Christian witness, works and words are not alternatives, they are partners. It is not enough for you to show the truth of the gospel by how you behave, you should also be prepared to speak about it.

TALK ABOUT JESUS

When Paul writes about 'the word of truth, the gospel of your salvation,' his choice of language is perfect. The Bible *is* 'the word of truth.' It tells us the truth about God, man, sin, heaven, hell, faith, holiness and about every other subject on which it speaks. Essentially it is 'the gospel of your salvation,' the good news that even the worst of sinners can get right with God. As Paul himself points out so clearly, God's good news is 'the gospel of God… *concerning his Son*' (Romans 1:1,3). The gospel is not based on philosophy, but on history, not on ideas, but on events, and those events centre on the Lord Jesus Christ. The purpose of evangelism is not to indoctrinate people with propositions, but to introduce them to a person. While talking to an unbeliever you may well find yourself touching on all kinds of religious issues, but always remember that at the end of the day what really matters is that you introduce the sinner to the Saviour. When Andrew met the Lord he immediately went to his brother and 'brought him to Jesus' (John 1:42). When Nathaniel questioned whether Jesus was really the Messiah, Philip simply invited him to 'Come and see' (John 1:46). Later, when he had the opportunity of speaking to a high-ranking Ethiopian politician who was reading the Old Testament in a search for the truth, Philip pointed him to Scripture and told him 'the good news about Jesus' (Acts 8:35). The story is told of two ferry boats passing each other on the Mississippi River. An old workman leaning on the rail of one of them pointed to the other boat and said to the passenger beside him, 'Look, there's the captain.' 'Yes,' replied the passenger, 'but why do you mention him?' 'Years ago,' said the workman, 'that man rescued me when I fell overboard, and ever since then I just loves to point him out!' As a Christian you should always be happy to point out the one who rescued you from sin and hell.

WHO WANTS TO BE A MARTYR?

The New Testament word 'witness' translates the original Greek word *martus* from which we get our English word 'martyr.' This is more than a hint to us that consistent Christian living and faithful Christian witness can be difficult and costly. For untold thousands of Christians, from New Testament times onwards, it has meant losing their lives. Far from this being a thing of the distant past, it has been said that more Christians were killed for their faith in the twentieth century than in any previous century in the church's history. In certain parts of the world today believers are executed, imprisoned, tortured, cut off from their families, socially suppressed, prevented from holding certain positions, or deprived of advanced education, solely because of their Christian commitment. These, too, are martyrs, and should find a constant place in our prayers. However, the Bible makes it clear that whole-hearted

Christian living and witness will always be costly in one way or another. Paul says that 'All who desire to live a godly life in Christ Jesus will be persecuted' (2 Timothy 3:12), and Jesus explains why this is so: 'If the world hates you, know that it has hated me before it hated you. If you were of the world, the world would love you as its own; but because you are not of the world, but I chose you out of the world, therefore the world hates you. Remember the word that I said to you: "A servant is not greater than his master." If they persecuted me, they will also persecute you' (John 15:18-20). Make sure you understand this! Difficulties you may face when you seek to live purely and witness faithfully are because 'you are not of the world.' When you became a Christian, you were 'delivered... from the domain of darkness and transferred... to the kingdom of his beloved Son' (Colossians 1:13). As a result, Satan began to deploy his spiritual agents against you, bringing opposition, criticism, misunderstanding, embarrassment, fear of ridicule, or other pressures to bear upon you, in a deliberate attempt to silence you—and far too often his tactics pay off. You may begin to think that spiritual subjects are too difficult to discuss with certain people, or that you might give offence, or that you might appear self-righteous. And to be honest, you may just be afraid of being thought some kind of religious freak; as the Bible says, 'The fear of man lays a snare' (Proverbs 29:25).

What should be your answer to this sort of thing? Begin by recognizing the reality of the situation. Settle for the fact that in seeking to witness you are working, 'behind enemy lines.' Realize that there are times when you will have to pay the price of being a Christian 'martyr.' And remember the promise Jesus made when he said, 'Blessed are you when others revile you and persecute you and utter all kinds of evil against you falsely on my account. Rejoice and be glad, for your reward is great in heaven, for so they persecuted the prophets who were before you' (Matthew 5:11-12).

THE VITAL WITNESS

In a court of law, there is sometimes a key witness whose evidence turns the whole course of a case. His words carry such weight that they constitute the decisive factor in the outcome of the proceedings. In the Christian life there is also a vital witness, whose influence is far more decisive—the Holy Spirit. Notice how perfectly Jesus times the appearance of this key witness in the New Testament. It was immediately after warning the disciples of the hatred and opposition they would face that Jesus adds, 'When the Helper comes, whom I will send to you from the Father, the Spirit of truth, who proceeds from the Father, *he will bear witness about me.* And you also will bear witness, because you have been with me from the beginning' (John 15:26-27). This may be the most important verse on the subject of witnessing in the whole of the New Testament. Left to ourselves, we would never be effective witnesses. No amount of eloquence, persuasion or argument will ever convince a single person of the truth of the Christian faith. We can only ever 'win a case' when the Holy Spirit's voice guides our thoughts and words. Jesus promises the early disciples that the Holy Spirit will 'convict the world concerning sin and righteousness and judgement' (John 16:8). Today, most people reject the witness of the Holy Spirit, just as most people rejected Jesus when they heard him in the flesh. Yet every day, in every corner of the world, as Christians bear faithful witness, the Spirit's voice is breaking through into the hearts and minds of unbelievers, enabling them to understand the truth about God, persuading them to admit their own condition and need, and drawing them to repentance and faith. This is exactly what happened to you when you became a Christian, and the day will come when you will see the fulfilment of the Bible's prophecy that God's world-wide family will be complete, and 'a great multitude that no one could number, from every nation, from all tribes and peoples and languages' will be 'standing before the throne and before the Lamb [*Jesus*]' (Revelation 7:9). This should be a tremendous encouragement to you as a Christian and as a witness for Christ. The work of Christ and the witness of the Spirit will not end in failure or disappointment, but in the glorious triumph of the salvation of all those who were chosen in Christ before the foundation of the world. To share in the trials of witnessing here and now will be to share in its triumph there and then.

Christians could not possibly have a greater incentive to witness. They also have a deeply personal motive. Reflect on what this is. Although you deserved eternal punishment, you have been given 'the free gift of God… eternal life in Christ Jesus our Lord' (Romans 6:23) and are assured of 'the promised eternal inheritance' (Hebrews 9:15). Yet you are surrounded by those who are not only spiritually blind (unable to see gospel truth) and spiritually deaf (unable to hear it) but spiritually dead. They may live respectable lives, but like all people they are 'by nature children of wrath' (Ephesians 2:3), just as you were before you became a Christian. They have 'no hope' (Ephesians 2:12), because as they are not trusting Christ for salvation they are heading for eternal disaster on 'the day of wrath when God's righteous judgement will be revealed' (Romans 2:5). Could you possibly have a greater motive to share with them 'the gospel of the grace of God' (Acts 20:24)?

17

WAITING, WATCHING AND WORKING

ONE OF THE most exhilarating things about the Bible is the way in which over and over again its history is proved to be astonishingly accurate. Sceptical scientists, archaeologists and historians have claimed flaws in its text, but none has been able to prove their case, and many experts in the same disciplines have often underlined its truth. But even confirmation of the Bible's history pales alongside another factor—the fulfilment of its prophecies. For instance, many prophecies about the nation of Israel made in the early part of the Old Testament were accurately fulfilled by the time the New Testament was written. Even more amazing is the way prophecies made about Jesus were fulfilled. It has been calculated that by the Law of Compound Probabilities, the odds against all the Old Testament prophecies about his birth, life, teaching, death, burial, resurrection and ascension being fulfilled are astronomical; to be precise, 6,451,444,325,125,601,253,342,971,930,704,920 to 1! Yet every single one was fulfilled to the letter in the space of thirty-three years. Included in these prophecies are twenty-five relating to his betrayal, death and burial. The odds against these alone being fulfilled are nearly 350 million to 1, yet they all took place exactly as prophesied within the space of twenty-four hours. Whatever clever arguments people may use in trying to disprove the Bible's record, they have to reckon with staggering facts.

THE FUTURE—NOW!

But that is not the end of the story. Not only does the Bible contain over 100 Old Testament prophecies about *the first* coming of Jesus into the world, the New Testament alone has about 300 references to his return, or *second* coming. Mathematically, this amounts to the subject being mentioned once for every thirteen verses from Matthew to Revelation. This is one of the most important, exciting and challenging truths in the whole Bible—and God has ensured that we should never be in any doubt about it. When the apostle Paul writes an encouraging letter to the church in Thessalonica, he reminds them that they have 'turned to God from idols to serve the living and true God, and to wait for his Son from heaven, whom he raised from the dead, Jesus who delivers us from the wrath to come' (1 Thessalonians 1:9-10). If he was the only New Testament writer that mentioned it, and did so many times, a sceptic might argue that the apostle had a bee in his bonnet (though even one mention in the Bible should be sufficient for the Christian). Yet it is difficult to find a New Testament writer who does *not* mention the subject.

Matthew records these words of Jesus: 'For the Son of Man is going to come with his angels in the glory of his Father' (Matthew 16:27).

Mark has the words of Jesus that men will one day 'see the Son of Man seated at the right hand of Power, and coming with the clouds of heaven' (Mark 14:62).

Luke includes the warning that 'The Son of Man is coming at an hour you do not expect' (Luke 12:40).

John has the plainest testimony of all, the straightforward promise of Jesus to his disciples that, having prepared a place for them in heaven, 'I will come again and will take you to myself, that where I am you may be also' (John 14:3).

The author of the letter to the Hebrews says of Jesus that 'having been offered once to bear the sins of many, will appear a second time, not to deal with sin but to save those who are eagerly waiting for him' (Hebrews 9:28).

James tells us that 'The coming of the Lord is at hand' (James 5:8).

Peter promises faithful Christians that 'when the chief Shepherd appears, you will receive the unfading crown of glory' (1 Peter 5:4).

The second coming of Christ is part of what the theologians call eschatology, or the doctrine of the last things, a subject full of controversy and differences of opinion. Countless books put forward various points of view about the exact timetable of events that will happen when the end of the world comes, and many people have become very hot under the collar insisting that their interpretation is the only right one. The Bible has been ransacked from cover to cover to find support for details of the terminal timetable, and organizations have even been raised up with the specific purpose of emphasizing one particular line of interpretation. All of this means that if you try to take in everything that is being said on the subject, you will find it very difficult to see the wood for the trees. In all of this confusion, the wisest thing is to keep to simple biblical guidelines. Scripture is always a better guide than even the most enthusiastic of speculations.

THE WORLD'S BEST-KEPT SECRET

One of the things the Bible teaches very firmly about the Second Coming of Christ is that no man knows when it will happen. Jesus said quite clearly that 'No one knows, not even the angels in heaven, nor the Son, but only the Father' (Mark 13:32). Yet ever since Jesus spoke those words, men have tried to forecast the date of the end of the world. Many people felt that it would happen in the year 1000. Others said it would happen in 1260. A brilliant mathematician calculated that Jesus would return between 1688 and 1700. A Roman Catholic priest wrote a book in which he forecast that the end of the world would come in 1847—and was promptly given permission to publish the book in 1848! The Jehovah's Witnesses have backed a whole string of losers— 1874, 1914, 1915 and 1975 are among the dates they earmarked for the great event. Yet all speculation on the subject is foolish and futile. For his own perfect reasons, God has chosen to keep the exact date of Christ's return a closely guarded secret.

SIGNS OF THE TIMES

Although nobody knows the day, month or year of Christ's return, the Bible has a kind of 'early warning system' which confirms the event. When asked what would be the signs of his return and of the end of the world, Jesus gave several replies. Here are some of them.

There will be an increase of false teaching: 'See that no one leads you astray. For many will come in my name, saying, "I am the Christ" and they will lead many astray... and many false prophets will arise and lead many astray' (Matthew 24:4-5,11). *There will be violent international conflicts*: 'you will hear of wars and rumours of wars . . . nation will rise against nation, and kingdom against kingdom' (Matthew 24:6-7). *There will be widespread natural disasters*: 'There will be famines and earthquakes in various places' (Matthew 24:7). *Christians will be persecuted and even killed for their faith*: 'Then they will deliver you up to tribulation and put you to death, and you will be hated by all nations for my name's sake' (Matthew 24:9). *Sin will worsen, leading many professing Christians to turn away from even their false faith*: 'Because lawlessness will be increased, the love of many will grow cold. But the one who endures to the end will be saved' (Matthew 24:12-13). *There will be world-wide evangelism*: 'And this gospel of the kingdom will be proclaimed throughout the whole world as a testimony to all nations, and then the end will come' (Matthew 24:14).

It would not be difficult to show that at almost any time during the last twenty centuries men could have ticked off almost all of these 'signs' and drawn the wrong conclusion that the world was nearing its end. Yet they have surely never seemed so obvious than in the day and age in which we now live? What we can be sure of is that the Second Coming of Christ is over 2,000 years nearer than when these prophecies were made. Jesus says, 'When you see these things taking place, you know that he is near, at the very gates' (Mark 13:29). If that was true then, it is more urgently true now. The Second Coming is never a doctrine for tomorrow, but always for today. What is more, it demands action. It is meant not just to add to our knowledge, but to affect our lives.

ARE YOU READY?

Many people dismiss all talk of Jesus coming again as sheer nonsense, but that, too, was predicted in the Bible. Peter writes that 'Scoffers will come in the last days with scoffing, following their own sinful desires. They will say, "Where is the promise of his coming? For ever since the fathers fell asleep, all things are continuing as they were from the beginning of creation"' (2 Peter 3:3-4). But for the Christian, what matters is not the voice of the sceptic, but the voice of the Saviour, who says, 'What I say to you, I say to all: "*Stay awake*"'(Mark 13:37). The challenge is simple and clear, and here are some of the ways to check your response.

You are not ready if you are lost. Jesus makes it clear that his return will be a moment of dramatic separation and terrifying judgement. Life will be going on as normal all over the world, with people 'eating and drinking, marrying and giving in marriage' (Matthew 24:38). Then suddenly he will appear, and in a moment of time, 'Two men will be in the field; one will be taken and one left' (Matthew 24:40-41). For Christians, it will be a moment of amazing delight as they are taken to be with their Saviour for ever. For unbelievers, it will be a moment of agonizing despair, as they realize they will have no further opportunity to get right with God, but are doomed to spend eternity in hell. Paul says that Jesus will return, 'in flaming fire, inflicting vengeance on those who do not know God and on those who do not obey the gospel of our Lord Jesus. They will suffer the punishment of eternal destruction, away from the presence of the Lord and from the glory of his might, when he comes on that day to be glorified in his saints, and to be marvelled at among all who have believed' (2 Thessalonians 1:8-10).

Here is the tremendous challenge that the Second Coming of Christ presents to the person who has never trusted him as their personal Saviour. This book has been written particularly to those who have recently become Christians and to help others grow in their faith—but are you sure where you stand on this issue? If you have never yet done so, then turn to God now in repentance and faith, so that if Jesus should return during your lifetime, you will be one of those received into heaven and not one of those condemned to spend eternity under God's terrible judgement.

You are not ready if you are lukewarm. While no true Christian can ever fall away and be lost, the Bible tells us that many who are living on the earth when Jesus returns will be embarrassed and ashamed by his sudden appearance, because of the sub-standard quality of their lives and their lack of loving devotion to him. John writes, 'And now, little children, abide in him, so that when he appears we may have confidence and not shrink from him in shame at his coming' (1 John 2:28). It is always awkward to meet someone with whom you have a lukewarm relationship—how much more so when that person is the Lord Jesus Christ! It is exactly here that the doctrine of the Second Coming is meant to motivate the Christian to godliness of life. After describing some of the global upheaval that will accompany Christ's return, Peter asks, 'What sort of people ought you to be in lives of holiness and godliness, waiting for and hastening the coming of the day of God' (2 Peter 3:11-12). If Jesus were to return today, would you be ashamed of your lack of devotion, your lukewarm love for him, your compromising or your backsliding?

You are not ready if you are lazy. In one of his parables, Jesus likens the kingdom of God to a nobleman who went abroad for a while, but promised to return. Before leaving, he entrusted each of his servants with a certain sum of money, with clear instructions; 'Engage in business until I come' (Luke 19:13). In exactly the same way, God has blessed every Christian in the world with particular gifts, talents, opportunities and responsibilities, and he expects them to be used to the full until Jesus returns. During my first visit to the United States I held a week of services at a church in

Michigan. On the first night, the choir opened the service with the song 'Coming again.' To my great surprise, they opened with the same song on the second night and then did the same on every night. I have never forgotten that. Whatever subject I preached on during that week, I felt it was against the background of the truth that Jesus is coming again, and that experience has been a constant reminder to me ever since that all of my Christian service should be done in the same context. The only way to be sure that you are actively involved in the Lord's service when he comes is to be involved in it *now*. The stewardship of the whole of your life should be seen in the light of the fact that his return will be unexpected and may be soon.

The Second Coming is not meant to make you frantic, but it should make you fervent; it should not produce recklessness, but it does demand carefulness. The Christian with a right view of the Bible's teaching on this great subject will learn to live in a spirit of watchful dedication, knowing that one day God 'will repay each person according to what he has done' (Matthew 16:27). In the light of this, I urge you to live a holy and committed life and to take every opportunity to tell others the good news of the gospel, with a sense of urgency as Christ's return draws ever closer.

18

'THE GREAT STORY'

Germany's Count Gottfried von Bismarck once said, 'Without the hope of eternal life, this life is not worth the effort of getting dressed in the morning,' but not everybody would agree with him. Life may have its ups and downs, pains and problems, doubts and difficulties, but for most people, regardless of whether they have any religious faith, these are easily outnumbered by other things—health and strength, warm personal friendships, food and drink, music, sport, seeing and hearing things they enjoy and discovering and using their personal gifts all play their part in making life worthwhile.

Yet for Christians, even the longest, fullest, most enriching and most enjoyable life is not the full story. There is much more (and much better) to come, and in *The Last Battle*, the final book in *The Chronicles of Narnia*, C S Lewis puts it perfectly. In the story, the Narnians leave Shadowlands (death) behind and as they move into the great lion Aslan's country things begin to happen that, in Lewis' words, 'were so great and beautiful that I cannot write them.' He then adds, 'And for us this is the end of all the stories, and we can most truly say that they all lived happily ever after. But for them it was only the beginning of the real story. All their life in this world and all their adventures in Narnia had only been the cover and the title page. Now at last they were beginning Chapter One of the Great Story which no one on earth has read; which goes on for ever; in which every chapter is better than the one before.'

This is Lewis' way of pointing us beyond the few years we spend on this planet to 'new heavens and a new earth' (2 Peter 3:13), the fulfilment of God's promise to the prophet Isaiah that at the end of time, 'I create new heavens and a new earth, and the former things shall not be remembered or come into mind' (Isaiah 65:17). The apostle John, in his God-given vision of the future, confirms that he saw 'a new heaven and a new earth, for the first heaven and the first earth had passed away' (Revelation 21:1).

As a Christian, you can be sure of being there, and this assurance is not based on emotions, hopes, longings, visions or dreams, but on God's promise to all who put their trust in the Lord Jesus Christ. As he died in your place and rose from the dead, giving dynamic proof that the penalty for your sins has been paid in full, so you may be sure that 'he [*God*] who began a good work in you will bring it to completion at the day of Jesus Christ' (Philippians 1:6).

It would be impossible to give even a sketchy outline here of what the Bible says about this, but I have set out its basic teaching in *The Hitch-hiker's Guide to Heaven*, published by EP Books. In this final chapter I want to adapt part of what I wrote there and to focus on the question, 'What will we be like when we are there?' In *The Last Battle*, C S Lewis wants us to see the great lion Aslan as a picture of Jesus, who is described in the Bible as 'the Lion of the tribe of Judah' (Revelation 5:5), and the apostle John answers our question in what could in context be the greatest words in the entire

Bible: *'we shall be like him, because we shall see him as he is'* (1 John 3:2).

SEEING THE SAVIOUR

On 2 June 1953 I was one of three million people who crowded London's streets to celebrate the Coronation of Queen Elizabeth II. I stood by the Victoria Memorial, directly in front of Buckingham Palace, and can still remember the excitement that swept through the crowds as the Gold State Coach left the palace forecourt and turned into The Mall on its way to Westminster Abbey. That was when I caught a first glimpse of my Queen, who had acceded to the throne on 6 February 1952 on the death of her father King George VI. Some three hours after that first sighting the excitement was even greater as she returned to the palace, this time formally crowned as sovereign. It was my supreme 'Kodak moment' and my tiny black and white photographs, taken with a primitive box camera, became treasured reminders of something I could never forget—*I had seen the Queen*!

Although I have never since seen her in person, my memory of 2 June 1953 is indelible. Yet I can join every other Christian in being certain of an experience infinitely more wonderful—seeing our Saviour! We will then see far more than even the disciples who lived in close company with Jesus for three years. The prospect of seeing the God-man Jesus Christ is not limited to prophets, church leaders, people of exceptional faith or outstanding Christian service. *All believers*, regardless of their standing, reputation or achievements here on earth, are included in the promise that John repeats when he sees in his vision of eternity that God's people 'will see his face' (Revelation 22:4).

People often have printed photographs or mobile phone

images of people that mean a great deal to them, but these are no substitutes for the much greater pleasure of seeing them face to face. Here on earth we can see only 'photographs' of Jesus as we read of him in the Bible. As we do, we should be amazed at his deity, the beauty of his character, the depth of his love and the wonder of his grace in rescuing us from the fate our sin deserved—yet we have a much greater joy to come when we see him face to face.

The story is told of a missionary working with a native convert on translating this part of the New Testament. When they came to the phrase 'we shall be like him' the native laid down his pen and cried, 'No! This is too much; let us write, "we shall kiss his feet."' His attitude is understandable, but we dare not edit the truth of God's promise that when we see our Saviour 'we shall be like him.' Emphasizing each word in turn should amaze us.

'we shall be like him'

As with the rest of the human race, we are by nature spiritually wrecked and bankrupt, with nothing good to be seen in us and not a good word to be said for us. Even at our best we continue to 'fall short of the glory of God' (Romans 3:23). At the height of his ministry as an apostle, Paul admits 'I know that nothing good dwells in me, that is, in my flesh' (Romans 7:18). He was not saying that his physical body was evil; the word 'flesh' here means his sinful nature. All Christians are born 'children of wrath, like the rest of mankind' (Ephesians 2:3), exposed to God's righteous anger and under his justified death sentence, so that left to ourselves we are destined to 'go away into eternal punishment' (Matthew 25:46). This makes God's promise, that we will spend eternity in 'new heavens and a new earth' and in a way beyond our imagination or understanding be like our glorified Saviour, so astonishing. This marvellous truth should motivate you to go on learning more and more about Jesus and to grow more like him, serving him as he deserves and demands, knowing the glorious future that awaits you.

'we *shall* be like him'

If John had written that being like Jesus for ever was a possibility (say as a reward for exceptional Christian living or outstanding service) it should still leave us amazed, as none of us would deserve this. But John goes infinitely further and says of all Christians that 'we *shall* be like him'—and does not allow a shadow of doubt to fall across the prospect.

The strongest confirmation of this is Paul's statement that all Christian believers are 'predestined to be conformed to the image of [*God's*] Son' (Romans 8:29). The word 'predestination' is made up from two Greek words, *pro* (before) and *horizo* (from which we get the word 'horizon', meaning a circular boundary). God has drawn a circle (a horizon) around all of those he has chosen and as that boundary is utterly secure, every person inside it will eventually be conformed to the likeness of Jesus. Paul underlines this security by adding, 'For I am sure that neither death nor life, nor angels nor rulers, nor things present nor things to come, nor powers, nor height nor depth, nor anything else in all creation, will be able to separate us from the love of God in Christ Jesus our Lord' (Romans 8:38-39).

'we shall be *like* him'

At the Second Coming, believers' bodies will be changed; Jesus will 'transform our lowly body to be like his glorious body' (Philippians 3:21). Just as the body he now has is no longer subject to earthly restrictions, so our bodies will no longer be subject to the limitations of time and space. They will never be subject to wear and tear, injury, illness or disease. Nor will they ever grow old or deteriorate in any way. As the American preacher John MacArthur says, 'You will never look and notice wrinkles or a receding hairline. You will never have a day of sickness. You won't be susceptible to injury or disease or allergies. There will be none of those things in heaven. There will only be absolute, imperishable perfection.' This explains why Paul tells us that while living on earth Christians long for 'the redemption of our bodies' (Romans 8:23). When Jesus returns, the bodies of believers will be raised from the dead and transformed into glorious, living bodies adapted for eternal life 'by the power that enables [*Jesus*] … to subject all things to himself' (Philippians 3:21).

Being like Jesus will mean not only physical but spiritual transformation, the ultimate fulfilment of God's plan for his people that they should be 'conformed to the image of his Son' (Romans 8:29). It is a genetic certainty that all children bear a resemblance to their parents, even if it is very slight and not immediately obvious. It is equally certain that in heaven we will not only have bodies that have the same qualities as that of our Saviour, but we will be spiritually transformed in such a way that in this sense, too, we will be *like* him.

'we shall be like *him*'

Even if we linked this promise solely to Jesus' earthly life it would be astonishing, as we saw in Chapter 3, he was 'without sin' (Hebrews 4:15) in every part of his life, but the New Testament fills in other details. His speech was such that people 'marvelled at the gracious words that were coming from his mouth' (Luke 4:22). He often met people who were driven by their egos, yet the Bible speaks of his 'meekness and gentleness' (2 Corinthians 10:1). He showed great composure under pressure; 'when he was reviled, he did not revile in return; when he suffered he did not threaten, but continued entrusting himself to him who judges justly' (1 Peter 2:23). He had a finely-tuned social conscience; when he saw people in need 'he had compassion on them' (Mark 6:34) and met their needs.

Yet this is only a shadow of what John is saying, because the picture John is holding before us is not Jesus in his earth-bound humanity, *but in his glorified humanity*— and we shall be like him! This does not mean that in heaven we will share the essential glory of Jesus as a member of the Godhead. We will not become divine, yet we will share in the glory given to Jesus Christ as the Saviour of sinners.

The Bible has so much more to say about Christians' eternal destiny, and I have unpacked some of this in the book I mentioned on page 108, but the American theologian Wayne Grudem makes a vital point:

> More important than all the physical beauty of the heavenly city, more important than the fellowship we will enjoy eternally with all God's people from all nations and all periods in history, more important than our freedom from pain and sorrow and physical suffering, and more important than reigning over God's kingdom—more important by far than any of these will be the fact that we will be in the presence of God and enjoying unhindered fellowship with him.

Can you imagine anything more glorious, more fulfilling, or more satisfying?

Now to him who is able to keep you from stumbling and to present you blameless before the presence of his glory with great joy, to the only God, our Saviour, through Jesus Christ our Lord, be glory, majesty, dominion and authority, before all time and now and for ever. Amen.

— JUDE 23-24